SOUTH PARK

THE SCRIPTS: BOOK TWO

**TREY PARKER
AND
MATT STONE**

First published in the UK in 2000 by Channel 4 Books
an imprint of Macmillan Publishers Ltd
25 Eccleston Place London SW1W 9NF
Basingstoke and Oxford

www.macmillan.co.uk

Associated companies throughout the world

ISBN 07522 7193 8

9 8 7 6 5 4 3 2 1

A CIP catalogue record for this book is available from the British Library.

Concept and Art Direction by Rob LaQuinta
Designed by Blackjacks
Printed in the EC

CONTENTS

EPISODE 206
THE MEXICAN STARING FROG OF SOUTHERN SRI LANKA

BY MATT STONE & TREY PARKER

INT. T.V. SET

A TITLE comes up: 'HUNTIN' and KILLIN'
with Jimbo and Ned.'

NARRATOR
And now back to Huntin' and Killin' with South Park's
favorite hunters Jimbo and Ned!

EXT. JIMBO AND NED'S PORCH - DAY

JIMBO
I'm Jimbo Kern and this here is Ned. Say hi, Ned.

NED
Hi, Ned.

JIMBO
HAAAAA!!! HAA-HAA!!! Now isn't that great?!

Jimbo looks to the camera guy who gives Jimbo a 'thumbs
up.' As Jimbo talks, titles come up: 'Pussy Law #4: No
animal shall be harmed even in self defense, unless
specific license and season is in order. Self defense
can only be justified by extreme provable peril
and or documented visible bodily harm.'

JIMBO
We have a terrific show for you today. We're gonna
kill some elk and we're gonna kill some mountain goats.
Now, the new law passed by Colorado legislature, which
Ned and I call Pussy Law Number FOUR - states that we
can no longer kill animals in self defense. In other
words, our old line of 'It's coming right for us...'

NED
It's coming right for us.

JIMBO
...No longer works. So now, we only kill animals
to, quote: 'thin out their numbers.' If we don't hunt,
then these animals will grow too big in number and
they won't have enough food. So you see? We have
to kill animals or else they'll die.

Jimbo and Ned have to just think about this one.
The camera guy scratches his head.

JIMBO
Uhh... So roll the tape.

EXT. SOUTH PARK - FOREST - DAY

We see a video image of Jimbo and Ned in full hunting gear.

JIMBO (V.O.)
Here we are up at Schaeffer's Crossing,
looking for some animals.

SOUTH PARK   PAGE 7

Scene 043 | Panel | BG

Location/Time

Dialogue

An- Animate one lowering
his neck eating.
2 of them. Should
blink one in the foreground
Should raise his head at us.

Action/Efx

A delicate grouping of five
deer stand around eating grass.

Trans. V.E.E.

Scene 044 | Panel | BG

Location/Time

Dialogue

JIMBO
Quick, Ned! THIN OUT THEIR NUMBERS!!!

Action/Efx

Trans. V.E.E.

Scene 044 cont. | Panel | BG

Location/Time

Dialogue

NED
THIN OUT THEIR NUMBERS!

Action/Efx

An- Ned walks out of
frame [Camera left.]

Trans.

Pg 3

SOUTH PARK   PAGE 20

Scene 045 | Panel | BG

Location/Time

Dialogue

An- tiptoe.

Action/Efx

V

Trans.

Scene 045 cont. | Panel | BG

FOOM!!

Location/Time

Dialogue

Action/Efx

Ned takes out his flame thrower and barbecues all five of
them.

Trans.

Scene 046 | Panel | BG

Location/Time

Dialogue

TO ONE Huge fire Cycle

Action/Efx

Trans.

Now we cut in to the video-taped Jimbo and Ned.

JIMBO
Lookie there, Ned! There's some deers!!

A delicate grouping of five deer
stand around eating grass.

JIMBO
Quick, Ned! THIN OUT THEIR NUMBERS!!!

NED
THIN OUT THEIR NUMBERS!

Ned takes out his flame thrower and barbecues all five
of them. Their little deer skeletons fall to the ground.

JIMBO
Good work, Ned! Now they won't starve!

EXT. JIMBO AND NED'S PORCH

Back to the set. The boys are horrified.

JIMBO
That sure was a great hunting trip.
We saved those deer from extinction.

NED
We're environmentalists.

JIMBO
Coming up next, were going to drop some napalm on an
unsuspecting family of beavers. And also try to thin out
the numbers of some endangered species.

EXT. SOUTH PARK ELEMENTARY - DAY

Establishing.

INT. CLASSROOM - DAY

Mr. Garrison walks over to the chalkboard
and writes 'Vietnam' in big letters.

Cartman raises his hand.

CARTMAN
Mr. Garrison, what's Vietnam?

MR. GARRISON
What's Vietnam... A question a child might ask,
but not a childish question...

Garrison laughs. Stan and Kyle look at
each other, confused.

MR. GARRISON
Children, for the next few days we'll be learning all
about Vietnam. Chances are that somebody in YOUR OWN
LIVES was affected by this incredible war.

MR. HAT
That's right, Mr. Garrison. The Vietnam War
was sticky and icky.

Kyle raises his hand.

KYLE
Mr. Garrison... Were YOU in Vietnam?

Garrison gets a very serious look. ZOOM IN to his
head, and the sounds of guns, screaming and
helicopters echo in his mind. This is all done
with archive footage of Vietnam.

The kids all watch, perplexed.

Garrison is in a trance, as the screaming and helicopter
sounds get louder and louder.

VOICE
Who's next to take a shower? Ooo! Me!!!

Suddenly, the sounds all come to a halt.
Garrison snaps out of his trance, smiling.

MR. GARRISON
(Matter-of-fact)
No, I wasn't in Vietnam. But sometimes
I like to pretend I was.
(Pause)
Anyway, children,
I'm going to assign you all a paper.

The kids all moan.

MR. GARRISON
I want you all to find somebody in your own life who was
in Vietnam, and interview them about it.

CLYDE
What if we don't know anybody who was in Vietnam?

MR. GARRISON
Then you get an F, fail the third grade, and have to get
a job cleaning septic tanks to support your drug habit.

CLYDE
Oh.

Stan turns to Kyle.

STAN
Dude, my uncle Jimbo was in Vietnam!

KYLE
Hey, yeah, he and Ned do that stupid T.V. show.

INT. T.V. SET

JIMBO
And now, time for Jimbo's mysteries of the unexplained.
One of our loyal viewers from South Park sent us some
eight millimeter film of what HE claims to be...
The Mexican Staring Frog of Southern Sri Lanka!

A video still picture of an artist's rendition of the frog.

JIMBO
Now as you all know, the Mexican staring frog of
Southern Sri Lanka can supposedly kill you with one
horrid gaze. If a person even so much as looks into the
frog's eyes, they can be paralyzed or even die! And this
film proves that the frog may very well exist!

The film begins.

EXT. FOREST - DAY

The camera shakes as if poorly hand-held.
We see some trees.

JIMBO
Now watch carefully, you're going to see
the Mexican Staring Frog...

After a few more seconds, a very brief, very faint blur
goes through the corner of the screen.

JIMBO
THERE! THERE! DID YOU SEE IT?!?!

EXT. JIMBO AND NED'S PORCH - DAY

JIMBO
ROLL THAT BACK AGAIN!!

EXT. FOREST - DAY

The same film, again we see the blur.

JIMBO
NOW FREEZE IT!!

It freezes into a bigger blur.

EXT. JIMBO AND NED'S PORCH - DAY

JIMBO
Well, I'd like to know what all you skeptics have
to say NOW!! What do you think Ned?

NED
I'm scared.

JIMBO
Well be sure to join us next time. Until then...
(singing)
We're so glad you spent your time with
us, while we slaughtered our way
through nature's guts, come again and
stay a while, we'll kill a lot more
living things and make them bleed.

NED
Good night!

The show ends.

CAMERA GUY
And we're... CUT!

CAMERA GUY
Great show guys.

Ned and Jimbo get up from their chairs and stretch.

JIMBO
Oh, lookie who's here! My little nephew Stanly!

The boys walk over.

JIMBO
So, you're interested in your Uncle Jimbo's
big T.V. show, huh?

STAN
No. We have to do a stupid report on Vietnam. You and Ned
are the only guys we know who were there.

JIMBO
Oh. Yeah, we sure were.

CARTMAN
Was it fun?

KYLE
Cartman! What kind of stupid ass question is that?!
Of course it was fun!

JIMBO
Well, sure, Vietnam was fun. But not like going to the
circus fun. Or fly-fishing in Montana fun. No, Vietnam
was more like shoving shards of broken glass up your ass
and then sitting in a tub of Tabasco sauce fun.

STAN
Woa.

JIMBO
Yepper, that's where me and Ned met...

DISSOLVE TO:

EXT. VIETNAM CAMP - THIRTY YEARS AGO

PAN ACROSS a very clichéd Vietnam scene.
Sixties music plays in the background,
as helicopters and troops walk round.

It is a scene reminiscent of Platoon. Except that as the
PAN continues, we see that there is also a merry-go-round,
a beautiful garden with flowers, and a jolly log ride.

JIMBO (V.O.)
I remember I had just gotten off the ferris wheel...

A younger Jimbo walks off a big colorful ferris wheel
in the middle of Camp.

JIMBO
Oh boy! What a gorgeous day!

A bird flies down and lands on Jimbo's shoulder.
It whistles a merry tune.

Jimbo whistles in return (like Snow White).

SERGEANT
KERNS! Get over here!

Jimbo walks over to a grouping of privates.

SERGEANT (cont'd)
The new privates are here.
I'm assigning one of them to you as a trainee.
NED Gerblanksi!

The privates part, and Ned steps out. He looks a little
different, he still has his arm and his beautiful voice.

NED
Ned Gerblanksi reporting, sir.

SARGEANT
Thanks Ned. The bad guys have been spotted about ten
clicks north of here. I know that you and Kern are
best suited to take them out. Are you up for it?

JIMBO AND NED
Sir yes SIR!

INT. HELICOPTER - VIETNAM

Ned and Jimbo are up in a helicopter.

                    JIMBO (V.O.)
        Soon, it was all on just me and Ned to
              win the war for America.

            Jimbo is piloting.

                    JIMBO
        Pass me some more cocoa, will you Ned?

                     NED
        Certainly. And would you like another muffin as well?

                    JIMBO
          Why the hell not, we're at war.

        Ned lights up yet another cigarette.

                    JIMBO
      Hey you know those things are bad for your throat.

                     NED
          No, that's all lies. I'll be fine.
            CHARLIES AT TWO O' CLOCK!!

        Down on the ground, THOUSANDS of
          Vietnamese scurry like ants.

                    JIMBO
           I see 'em! Drop the bomb!

                     NED
          THE BOMB'S NOT RELEASING!!

                    JIMBO
                   Oh no!

                     NED
               It won't budge!!

                    JIMBO
        Then we have only one option...

        Jimbo points the chopper downward and
              zooms towards the ground.

                     NED
        What are you doing, man?

                    JIMBO
      We have to take 'em out Ned! At all costs!!
          Die you red commie bastards!!!

        The chopper hurls towards the Vietnamese. Ned grabs
        Jimbo's hand as death flies toward them.

        CRASH!!! The chopper slams into a bunch
              of Vietnamese soldiers.

Jimbo and Ned jump out from the wreckage, shooting in all directions. Vietnamese die all over the place.

Finally, Ned is out of bullets. He pulls out a grenade, pulls the pin and BAM!! It takes Ned's arm right off.

NED
YAAGHGH!!!

Jimbo empties his gun.

JIMBO
Oh, no! Out of ammo!

He draws a large elegant sword,
then spots a mighty white stallion.

Ned, meanwhile, uses martial arts expertly
to fend off his Vietnamese attackers.

Jimbo jumps onto the white steed and starts
chopping up victims with his sword.

Ned is like Chuck Norris.

Finally, all the Vietnamese lie dead.

JIMBO
WE DID IT, NED! WE KILLED THE ENTIRE VIET CONG ARMY!

Ned looks over the horizon, where he see
thousands of dead bodies.

NED
Whoopee!

Ned lights a smoke.

JIMBO
Let's get back to base camp! We can ride the
log ride before it closes!

Ned jumps on the back of the horse and the
two ride off into the sunset.

EXT. JIMBO AND NED'S PORCH

JIMBO
And that's the way it happened, boys.

STAN
Wow!

CARTMAN
Man, Vietnam was sweet!

PRODUCER
Great news guys! Your T.V. show ratings have doubled!

JIMBO
WOW!

PRODUCER
They've gone from SIX people to TWELVE!

JIMBO
Holy smokes! We could get an Emmy!

EXT. SOUTH PARK PUBLIC ACCESS - DAY

People are getting ready to shoot on the Jesus and Pals set.

PRODUCER
We've got to do it, J. Your ratings are being killed
by the Jimbo and Ned Hunting Show.

JESUS
But I don't really care about that.

PRODUCER
Well you BETTER care, Mr. Smarty Pants. No ratings
means no show. If you want to keep reaching out to people,
you have to keep up with the times.

JESUS
Oh, alright...

AD
Alright, we're 10 seconds to air guys-

PRODUCER
Remember: big, Big, BIG!!!!

She runs off leaving Jesus looking pretty
uncomfortable on stage.

AD
AND FIVE... FOUR... THREE...

A BAND kicks in with some funky music and
spotlights circle the studio. SLICK GRAPHICS
spin into frame with a big WHOOSH!

ANNOUNCER
It's your hour of power on mid-day mountain cable
access. Put your hands together and welcome,
the ONLY man in town who always has a FULLY stocked
wine cellar... JESUS CHRIST!

The band ends with flourish. Fireworks go off behind
the set. Jesus looks around a little confused.

JESUS
Uh... hi.

The producer motions to Jesus to keep it going.

                    JESUS
              Uh... yeah, okay -

Jesus reads straight from his note cards.

                    JESUS
- Beginning today, we're taking the show in a new
direction. We've got some VERY interesting people
coming on the show this week for YOU, our viewers.
Today's guest is T.V.'s Gilligan... MR. BOB DENVER!

A Tonight Show like entrance for happy
jolly little Bob Denver. They sit down.

                  ANNOUNCER
              Here's Bob Denver.

                    JESUS
               Hi Bob Denver.

                  BOB DENVER
           Hi Jesus! Great to be here!
        An awkward silence. LONG silence.

                    JESUS
         So Bob... So you just get in town?

                  BOB DENVER
                Yes. Just got in.

           Another awkward silence.

                    JESUS
         So... So what've you been up to?

                  BOB DENVER
          Nothing. Nothing really at all.

Yet another long beat. The Producer makes a gesture
and the band starts playing 'Nothing from Nothing.'

              Jesus looks around.

                    JESUS
                  Oh boy.

INT. CLASSROOM.

Stan, Kyle, Kenny, and Cartman are up in front of the
class. Stan reads from notecards.

                    STAN
...and after killing the entire Viet Cong army, they
returned to base camp. Once there, they rode the
Devil's drop roller coaster and ate cotton candy.
And ultimately, Ned got the purple heart for his
courageous defense of the log ride.

Garrison rolls his eyes.

STAN
So was the horror of Vietnam. The end.

BOYS
The end.

KYLE
Are there any questions?

Garrison raises his hand.

KYLE
Yes Mr. Garrison?

MR. GARRISON
Yes, where in the fuck did you hear this
ridiculous load of bullshit?

STAN
From Vietnam veterans.

MR. GARRISON
Well boys, its obvious to me that you didn't do your work,
and then you stayed up all night making up some
ridiculous lie.

STAN
No, no we didn't.

MR. GARRISON
You all receive an F MINUS.

KYLE
F minus? Can he do that?

STAN
(shocked)
But we're not making it up...

MR. GARRISON
Stanly, the Vietnam War was a WAR! There weren't
galloping steeds or singing birds or log rides.

KYLE
How do you know? You weren't even there.

MR. GARRISON
Well that's it! All of you have detention
for the rest of the week.

BOYS
AWW!!

FIRST COMMERCIAL BREAK.

ACT II

INT. CAFETERIA - AFTER SCHOOL

Mr. Mackey sits at the front of the room with a big sign
that says 'DETENTION: QUIET!!!!!'

The boys sit with their hands crossed
and talk in a whisper.

MR. MACKEY
Welcome to detention, Okay? Mr. Garrison told me about
your little joke. It is important for you to know
WHY you are in detention for you to obtain the full
benefits from it. You are here because you are inferior,
okay? You are here because you are awkward, okay?...

Mr. Mackey continues.

CARTMAN
Well Stan, thanks a lot for having such a cool uncle
that got us all detention for a week.

KYLE
Yeah dude, your uncle Jimbo sucks ass!

MACKEY
Ssshh, okay?!

Mackey shushes the boys. They wait a beat.

STAN
Why would he just invent a story instead of
just telling us the truth?

CARTMAN
Well, let's see maybe 'cuz he's an old
drunk hillbilly dick!

MACKEY
SSSSHH, okay?!

KYLE
We got to get him back dude.

CARTMAN
Totally.

STAN
How?

KYLE
Well, he screwed us by making something up...
I say we do the same thing.

STAN
Well, what do you mean?

KYLE
Did you ever see that one Brady Bunch where the guy...

CARTMAN
Oh yeah sweet, sweet!

The boys all lean in to hear Kyle's whispering.

ACT II

ANGLE - TELEVISION

ANNOUNCER
And now back to 'Huntin' and Killin'' with South Park's
favorite hunters - Jimbo and Ned!

EXT. JIMBO AND NED'S PORCH

Jimbo and Ned are on camera again.

JIMBO
Welcome hunters! Boy have we got a show for you today!
We have just received a tape from ANOTHER viewer
who filmed the Mexican Staring Frog of Southern
Sri Lanka RIGHT HERE IN SOUTH PARK!!

NED
Agh!

JIMBO
Yes, now we're about to roll the film, but remember, if
you look the Mexican Staring Frog in the eyes, you can
go catatonic. We don't know if this applies to PICTURES
of the frog or not, but who wants to take chances?
So when we roll this film, be sure to look away.

Jimbo and Ned cover their eyes and look away
from the video screen.

JIMBO
Okay, roll the film, Tom!

FOOTAGE of an obviously fake little frog sitting
on a front porch. It just sits there. For a long
time. It doesn't move.

Jimbo and Ned keep their eyes off it.
The camera guy looks away as well.

JIMBO
Is it over?

Jimbo sneaks a look at the screen
just as the image disappears.

JIMBO
Okay, it's over.

THE MEXICAN STARING FROG OF SOUTHERN SRI LANKA

Everyone goes back to normal.

JIMBO
Well, there you have it. Undeniable PROOF that the Mexican Staring Frog of Southern Sri Lanka exists!!!! And you saw it HERE on the Jimbo and Ned show!

INT. KYLE'S HOUSE - DAY

The boys are all on the couch watching the show.

KYLE
Dude! I can't believe they fell for it!

STAN
Yeah what a couple of dumbasses!

KENNY
Mph rmph rm rmph rmph rm!

The boys all laugh.

STAN
Yeah!

KYLE
Come on, we gotta go make another one!

The boys all head out the door.

CARTMAN
Lying kicks ass!

INT. JESUS AND PALS SET

The crew is down during a commercial break.

PRODUCER
Jesus!

JESUS
Yeah?

Jesus is getting his face powdered.

PRODUCER
We're in trouble. The Jimbo and Ned show made up some ridiculous staring frog story and jumped another two points in the ratings!

JESUS
Oh, oh. So what are we supposed to do?

PRODUCER
I don't know. We'll have to continue with the changes we've made, and then go even further...

CAMERA GUY
And we're back in FIVE, FOUR, THREE -

PRODUCER
Remember, BIG BIG BIG!!!

Ricki Lake music starts as the Jesus and Pals
logo glides past the frame.

Jesus is in the audience a la Ricki.

JESUS
If you're just joining us, we've been listening to
Michelle's incredible story of survival. Go on, Michelle.

WOMAN GUEST
(in tears)
Well, as I was saying, I tried and tried but the
overturned car just wouldn't budge. My husband
was trapped for twelve hours.

JESUS
And yet somehow he managed to survive.

WOMAN GUEST
That's right. He's a very brave man and I love him very much.

The man guest smiles at the woman. His head is flat like
a pancake and his arm sticks out of his back.

MAN GUEST
I lov oo too.

JESUS
Well, let's see if the audience has any questions.
(beat)
Yes, you over there-

Jesus trots over to a large ugly woman.

WOMAN
I think she needs to kick him to the curb, baby!

Jesus looks confused.

JESUS
Kick WHO to the curb?

WOMAN
Her no good husband!! She's gotta lose that
zero and get herself a hero!!!

The crowd goes wild.

JESUS
But -

Another woman stands up next to her.

WOMAN 2
He wants to have his cake and eat it too! He's gotta
dump that trash, girlfriend! It's all about respect!
You gotta have respect for yourSELF!

The woman guest looks extremely confused.

JESUS
Uh... I think we've somewhat missed the point here,
let's go to somebody else...

Jesus goes to another audience member.

JESUS
Yes, your comments?

BLACK MAN
Montel, I think we're forgetting something very
important in all of this. Okay, sure he touched
some children, but the man is a great singer
and he has entertained us for so many years.

JESUS
What are you talking about?

BLACK MAN
Michael Jackson. All this bad mouthing and putting the
man down. Maybe he did touch some children now and then,
but come on! It's Michael Jackson. Michael Jackson!

People applaud. Jesus pulls the mike away from the man.

JESUS
Uh... We'll be back right after these messages...

EXT. SOUTH PARK FOREST - DAY

Kyle has a video camera.

STAN
Ready you guys?

KYLE AND CARTMAN
Ready!

STAN
Okay? ACTION!!

EXT. SOUTH PARK FOREST - CAMERA - DAY

Through an unsteady videocamera, we see a blurry picture
of a small bush in the forest.

Suddenly, it starts to shake slightly.

Then, a dark blur appears at one side of the screen
behind the bush. It hops a couple of times.

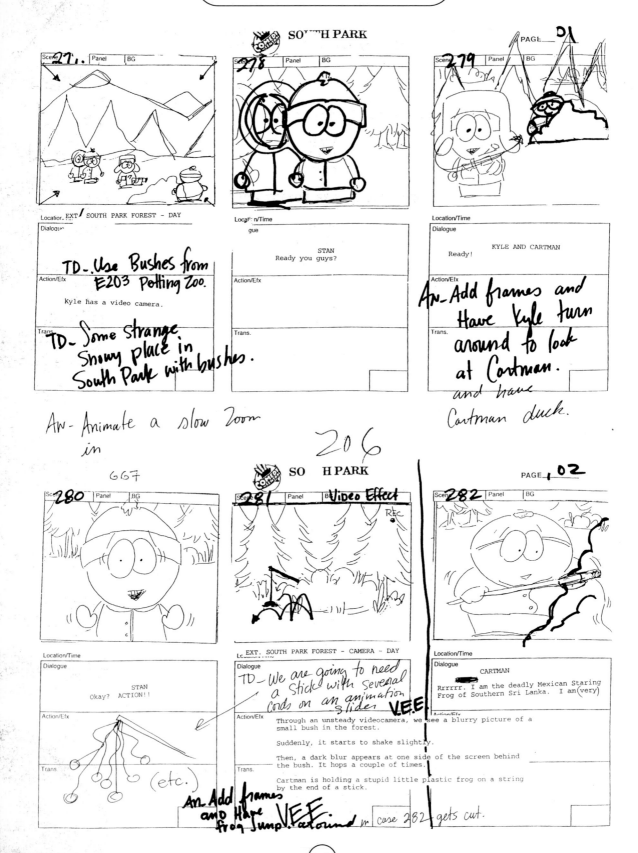

SOUTH PARK

Scene 277. Panel | BG

Location. EXT / SOUTH PARK FOREST - DAY

Dialogue

TD - Use Bushes from E203 Petting Zoo.

Action/Efx

Kyle has a video camera.

Trans.

TD - Some strange snowy place in South Park with bushes.

AW - Animate a slow Zoom in

GG7

Scene 278 Panel | BG

Location/Time

gue

Dialogue

STAN
Ready you guys?

Action/Efx

Trans.

PAGE — 01

Scene 279 Panel | BG

Location/Time

Dialogue

KYLE AND CARTMAN
Ready!

Action/Efx

AW - Add frames and Have Kyle turn around to look at Cartman. and have Cartman duck.

Trans.

206

SOUTH PARK

Scene 280 Panel | BG

Location/Time

Dialogue

STAN
Okay? ACTION!!

Action/Efx

Trans.

(etc.)

AW Add frames and Have frog jump. VEE. around in case 282 gets cut.

Scene 281 Panel | BG **Video Effect**

REC

EXT. SOUTH PARK FOREST - CAMERA - DAY

Dialogue

TD - We are going to need a stick with several cords on an animation slider VEE

Action/Efx

Through an unsteady videocamera, we see a blurry picture of a small bush in the forest.

Suddenly, it starts to shake slightly.

Then, a dark blur appears at one side of the screen behind the bush. It hops a couple of times.

Cartman is holding a stupid little plastic frog on a string by the end of a stick.

Trans.

PAGE — 02

Scene 282 Panel | BG

Location/Time

Dialogue

CARTMAN
Rrrrrr. I am the deadly Mexican Staring Frog of Southern Sri Lanka. I am (very)

Action/Efx

Trans.

THE MEXICAN STARING FROG
OF SOUTHERN SRI LANKA

Cartman is holding a stupid little plastic frog on a
string by the end of a stick.

CARTMAN
(O.S.)
Rrrrrr. I am the deadly Mexican Staring Frog of
Southern Sri Lanka. I am very scary and dangerous!

STAN
(O.S.)
CUT!

EXT. SOUTH PARK FOREST - DAY

STAN
Cartman!

CARTMAN
What?!

STAN
It's supposed to be a frog!

CARTMAN
I know that!

STAN
Since when do frogs talk, Cartman?

CARTMAN
It's a Sri Lankan frog!

KYLE
Der, Cartman!

CARTMAN
Der yourself, hippie!

KYLE
JUST DO IT AGAIN, CARTMAN, AND DON'T MAKE IT TALK!!

STAN
Ok, here we go. Ready?

KYLE
Are you ready, Cartman?

CARTMAN
I'm ready, Steven Spielberg!

STAN
Action!

Cartman sloppily bounces his little frog up and down.

CARTMAN
Rrrr... Screw you guys...

SO~~UT~~H PARK

Scene **291** | BG **SIA285**

Location/Time

Dialogue

CARTMAN
Der yourself, hippie!

Action/Efx

Trans.

SO~~UT~~H PARK

Scene **292** | Panel | BG **SIA290**

Location/Time

Dialogue

KYLE
JUST DO IT AGAIN, CARTMAN, AND DON'T MAKE
IT TALK!!

Action/Efx

Trans.

SOUTH PARK **p. 106**

Scene **293** | Panel | BG **SIA280**

Location/Time

Dialogue

STAN
Ok, here we go. Ready?

Action/Efx

294 is
cut

Trans.

SIA 281 Add Cart~~man~~
Video Effect.

Scene **295** | ~~Panel~~ | BG

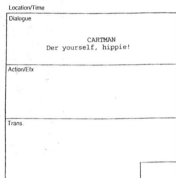

O REC

Location/Time

Dialogue
KYLE
Are you ready, Cartman?

CARTMAN
I'm ready, Steven Spielberg!

Action/Efx _____

Cartman sloppily bounces his little frog up and down.

Trans.

SO~~UT~~H PARK

Scene **295 contd.** | | BG

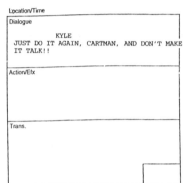

• Rec.

Location/Time

Dialogue

STAN
Action!

Action/Efx

Trans. **Add frames to**
this. Add hand held
shake look to
it. This will also
be used as 313
(see how many frames it is)

Scene **296** | Panel | BG **48 frames**

Location/Time **go.**
(wider than shown)

Dialogue

Action/Efx

Send 48 frames
of the town
establishing shot.

Trans.

No Animation

EXT. SOUTH PARK AVENUE

CARTMAN
Why do I have to dress up like the old lady?!

Indeed, Cartman has a little gray wig and a dress on.
Kyle has a video camera.

KYLE
Cuz old lady's are fat and you are too!

CARTMAN
Ech, Goddammit!

STAN
Come on Cartman, the way we're shooting this,
nobody will ever know it's you.

CARTMAN
They better not!

STAN
Okay, when I yell action, you start to walk this way,
then Kenny's going to pull the plastic frog in
front of you and you have to be scared -

CARTMAN
Scared? Of a plastic frog?

STAN
It's ACTING Cartman. You have to pretend you're
really scared then the Mexican Staring Frog
will look you in the eyes, then you fall down
like you're dead, okay? Ready?

CARTMAN
Man this is stupid.

STAN
Good, and... ACTION!

EXT. JIMBO AND NED'S

JIMBO
Well, it appears as though a lot of you SKEPTICS thought
that the film we showed of the Mexican Staring Frog of
Southern Sri Lanka was a FAKE. They say it didn't HARM
anybody... Well, it just so happens that we just received
ANOTHER film from ANOTHER anonymous viewer! ROLL IT!

The shitty little film that the boys made appears on the
screen. The stupid plastic frog bounces through frame.

It then cuts to Cartman as the old lady
who sees the frog, and then passes out.
Then we see Kenny moon the camera.

JIMBO
There you go! PROOF that not only is this frog REAL, but
it is doing harm to people of South Park AS WE SPEAK!!

NED
Damn that frog.

JIMBO
Well that does it! All this week Ned and I will
be risking life and limb as we go on location to
HUNT THE MEXICAN STARING FROG OF SOUTHERN SRI LANKA!
Join us won't you?

INT. JESUS AND PALS SET

Jesus' producer is watching the Jimbo and Ned on her
monitors. Her head falls into her hands.

PRODUCER
Oh no, no, no! This is the biggest publicity stunt
I've ever seen. Damn those hunters are clever!

JESUS
Uh... Clever?

PRODUCER
It's genius, it really is. Hell, I even want to watch
them hunt the Mexican Staring Frog! Unless...

JESUS
Unless what?

PRODUCER
Unless we can prove to the world that the whole
thing is a sham. If we prove that the Mexican
Staring Frog of Southern Sri Lanka is just something
made up by Jimbo and Ned, we can have them taken
off the air. Perhaps even KILLED!

JESUS
Look, why don't we stick to our own show.
People will watch again.

PRODUCER
Oh J... You are so Omnipotent and yet so naive...
We'll launch a full investigation. And in the meantime
we can cash in on the video tapes.

JESUS
What video tapes?

INT. JESUS AND PALS SET

Jesus is sitting at his chair.

JESUS
Yea, my children. I am the way and the
light. Let's get to our next guest...

As Jesus continues, a loud voiceover begins.

NARRATOR
You've seen Jesus and Pals... Now you've got to get the
video! Jesus and Pals is too hot for TV!

Clip of Jesus watching a man spray whipped cream
on a topless woman.

NARRATOR (cont'd)
Things get a little outta control!

NARRATOR (cont'd)
You won't believe your eyes!!

Two women in bikinis take off their tops as 'TOO HOT'
censor bars cover their chests.

NARRATOR (cont'd)
Order now, only $19.95!! Remember, this
is stuff you CAN'T see on TV!!!!

A number and address to call appears on the screen.

The commercial ends.

ACT III

EXT. SOUTH PARK AVENUE

The Jimbo and Ned crew is driving in the van.

JIMBO
Anonymous tip?

CAMERA GUY
Yeah, it was left on our answering machine. All it
said was that they saw the Mexican Staring Frog
just south of Stark's pond this morning.

JIMBO
Hey Ned, remember that time we got an
anonymous tip back in Nam?

CAMERA GUY
You were in Nam? Where were you stationed?

NED
DeNang.

CAMERA GUY
With the log ride?

JIMBO
Yup.

CAMERA GUY
Man, I was in Tet. We had a badass roller coaster.

But all we ever wanted was a log ride... We waited
and we waited... But they never built us one.

Jimbo and Ned look sad as they listen to the tale.

CAMERA GUY
I think Danforth wanted a log ride more than
anybody but he... He had to settle with that
lame dinosaur water adventure ride...

The camera guy breaks down and starts crying.

Jimbo puts a hand on the camera guy's shoulder.

JIMBO
That war was hell on everybody.

PRODUCER
(talking on his cell phone)
Good... Okay, okay. Bye.
(hanging up)
Great news everybody! This weeks ratings are
through the roof! We're up to TWENTY people!

JIMBO
Wow! Do we get more money?

PRODUCER
No, but I do! We're now THE highest
rated show on Mountain Cable Access!
God bless the Mexican Staring Frog!!!

EXT. SOUTH PARK - FOREST - DAY

The boys are gathered in the forest. Kyle puts
the little plastic frog on a large rock in the
middle of a clearing.

KYLE
Dude, they are gonna look SO stupid!

CARTMAN
Totally!

STAN
They deserve it for lying to us dude.

CARTMAN
Revenge is so very, very sweet.

The ROAR of an engine.

STAN
They're here! Hurry and hide!

The boys jump behind a bush as Jimbo and Ned
and the camera crew pull up.

JIMBO
Let's hunt!

PRODUCER
We'll start with a two-shot of you and Ned
getting your equipment together and -

NED
- Jimbo, look.

Ned points to a rock behind them all where the little
plastic frog sits motionless.

JIMBO
HIT THE DECK!!!

Everybody jumps to the ground.

PRODUCER
What is it?

JIMBO
It's him! The Mexican Staring Frog of Southern Sri Lanka!
He's right over there on that rock!

PRODUCER
He is?

The producer peers up over the rock.

Jimbo quickly yanks his head back down.

JIMBO
Dumbass! You've GOT to keep your eyes away from him!
STAY DOWN! Ned, you take flank position, I'll try
and keep it turned away from you.

NED
Roger that.

JIMBO
(into camera)
Hello fellow hunters. Have we got a show for you
today! The Mexican Staring Frog is sunning
itself on a rock directly behind us.

Ned runs around and hides behind a tree, making sure
the whole time not to look at the little plastic frog.

JIMBO
We've got to take the frog by surprise.

Jimbo takes out a grenade.

JIMBO
I'm going to create a diversion using this incendiary
device, while Ned will ambush him from the rear.

Jimbo throws the bomb over his shoulder. BOOOOM!
It blows a huge hole in the ground right
next to the little plastic frog.

JIMBO
NOW NED! HE'S NOT LOOKING!!!

Ned rushes in with the flamethrower.

JIMBO
QUICK NED! HIT HIM WITH THE SHOTGUN! NOW NED!!!

Nothing. No sound.

JIMBO
Ned?!... Ned????

Jimbo peeks over to the rock.
Ned stands a few feet from the frog, not moving.

JIMBO
Oh no...

Ned is caught in the gaze of the frog. Little concentric
circles surround his eyes. He drops his gun.

NED
Zzzzzz...

JIMBO
Come on Ned buddy, snap out of it!

But Ned is catatonic. He can't move at all.

JIMBO
Come back to me buddy!!

PRODUCER
(to camera guy)
You getting all this?

The camera guy nods.

JIMBO
(to camera)
Hold onto your butts...

Jimbo jumps up with his gun and BLASTS
the little plastic frog off the rock.

JIMBO
TAKE THAT YOU DEMON FROG!!!

Ned is still catatonic. Jimbo shakes him.

JIMBO
Ned?! Ned?! Can you hear me?!

THE MEXICAN STARING FROG OF SOUTHERN SRI LANKA

                    JIMBO
Quick! Somebody call an ambulance! This man is catatonic!

                    PRODUCER
        Get the Flight for Life helicopter!

The kids all climb out of the bushes.

                    STAN
              Holy crap, dude.

EXT. HOSPITAL - DAY

              Establishing.

INT. HOSPITAL - DAY

Jimbo is sitting beside Ned's bed reading a book. Ned is still catatonic. The Producer is standing off to the side.

                    JIMBO
                   (Reading)
        But Pony Boy was beat up pretty bad.
          He kept saying 'Stay Gold.'

Jimbo closes the book.

                    JIMBO
Aw, Ned... If you can hear me... You gotta snap out of it.
    'Cause if you don't, I'll never forgive myself.

Ned is still catatonic.

The boys walk in to find Jimbo drying his tears.

                    JIMBO
              Oh, Stanly! He's gone!
        My only friend in the world is gone!

                    STAN
Dude! He's okay! That frog wasn't even real!

                    STAN
                   Look-

Stan holds up another plastic frog.

                    JIMBO
        AGH!! What the hell are you doing?!
          I almost looked right at that!!

                    STAN
Dude, it's just a plastic frog. It's not real. Check it out -

He hands the frog to Jimbo. Jimbo examines it.

                    JIMBO
                  ...What?

31

                              STAN
          We shot all those videos and sent them in.

                              KYLE
          Yeah, we made the whole thing up.
          It was all just a really really funny joke.

                             JIMBO
             You sent in those videos?!!!!

                            PRODUCER
             Oh, this is not good.

                             JIMBO
          My best friend is a vegetable and I'm going
          to be the laughing stock of South Park!

                              KYLE
             Aw come on! Ned's faking it!
          That frog was just a piece of plastic.

                              STAN
          Yeah, come on Ned, quit faking!

                             JIMBO
          You boys don't understand. Ned was so freaked out
          by the idea of the Mexican Staring Frog that
          he must have sent himself into a deep coma!
          Stan and Kyle look at each other, concerned.

                          VOICE (O.S.)
             It's a psychosomatic response.

          We PAN over to the doorway where the Jesus and
             Pal's producer is standing just outside
             the room holding one of those telescopic
          microphones that is used in football games.

                            PRODUCER
       I couldn't help overhearing your conversation just now.

                 The producer walks in.

                              KYLE
                    Who are you?

                            PRODUCER
       I produce a little TV show called Jesus and Pals. You
       might have heard of it. Your story is AMAZING! Full of
         jealousy, duplicity, backstabbing and bitterness!

                             JIMBO
                    Uh... thanks?

                            PRODUCER
       How would you like to share your remarkable story
             with us on tomorrow's show?

INT. TELEVISION STUDIO

CHEESY MUSIC. Lights search the crowd.
Superimposed titles read 'Tots in Trouble!'

Jimbo and the boys are on stage.
Ned sits next to Jimbo, still catatonic.

JESUS
We're back with Jimbo and his nephew Stan.
These kids can't stop lying, can they?

JIMBO
That's right Jesus. No respect for their elders.
As some of you may know, I host a local show on hunting-

A smattering of applause.

JIMBO
Thanks. We've been hunting the Mexican Staring Frog
for a week based on some video footage we received
from a viewer. Well, it turns out that these kids
FAKED the footage!

JESUS
Is this true, Stan?

STAN
It was just a joke.
We didn't think it would hurt anybody.

Jesus looks at the producer who signals for a commercial.

JESUS
We'll find out more about this debauchery when we return!

Music kicks in and the camera BOOMS off Jesus.

AD
And we're... OUT!

Producers rush the stage.

PRODUCER
You're corpses up here!!
We need A LOT more action from everybody!

JIMBO
Like what?

PRODUCER
Like go ahead and tell how your nephew
Stan takes drugs and worships Satan.

JIMBO
Satan. Got it.

STAN
Whoa, I don't take drugs and worship Satan! That's lying!

JIMBO
Give you a taste of your own medicine you little fibber!

PRODUCER
And you kids! I didn't bring you on
this show to be boring! Somebody get
pissed and throw a chair at Ned here.

CARTMAN
Dibs!

PRODUCER
Remember, you all start to fight after
the chair is thrown. That's your cue!

JIMBO
Righty.

Music kicks in. The audience goes wild.

JESUS
Welcome back to Jesus and Pals! Jimbo,
why do you think little Stanly lies?

JIMBO
I'll tell you why... Because he's on
drugs and he worships the devil!!!

The crowd GASPS! Stan sits in shock.

AUDIENCE
JESUS!!! JESUS!!!! JESUS!!!

JESUS
Wow.

JESUS
Now Stanly, it sounds like your uncle
is really worried about you.

STAN
Well... I only did it because he molested me!!!

GASP!!! Jesus' jaw drops.
Two producers high-five behind the camera.

JIMBO
Why you little piece of crap!

STAN
You big piece of crap!!

CARTMAN
That's it, now I'm all pissed off!!!

Cartman picks up a chair and wings it at Ned. It hits him on the head but he doesn't move an inch.

                    CARTMAN
                Take that hippie!

                    JIMBO
                    HEY!!!

He picks up his chair and throws it at Stan. Stan ducks and it hits a lady in the crowd.

                    AUDIENCE
                JESUS!!! JESUS!!!!

                    JESUS
            Okay, okay. That's enough!

She dashes up and attacks Jimbo.

                LADY IN THE CROWD
                TAKE THAT YOU ASSHOLE!!!

                LADY IN THE CROWD
                What the fuck was that?!

                    JESUS
        Uh, let's watch the language people -

                    JIMBO
            BRING IT ON YOU BITCH!!!

                    CARTMAN
        HEY GET OFF OF HIM YOU FUCKIN' NUT SACK!!!

Cartman jumps on them. The crowd jumps on the boys. A huge melée ensues.

                    KENNY
                    Mrph mrph!!

Two angry crowd members have Kenny between them in a tug of war. They tug and tug.

                    JESUS
        Let's all make our way back to our seats.

                    KENNY
                    MMMMRPPH!!

They RIP him in half, killing him instantly.

                    STAN
            OH MY GOD! THEY KILLED KENNY!!!

                    KYLE
                YOU BASTARDS!!!

                              JESUS
             Let's all make our way back to our seats.

           No one notices. The fights continue.

     Full-on chaos. The dialogue is a continuous BLEEEP.

                              JESUS
                       SHUT THE FUCK UP!!!!

            Silence. Everyone looks at Jesus.

                              JESUS
             Jesus, what is wrong with you people!?

     People look ashamed. Everyone disentangles themselves
                 from their respective piles.

                              JESUS
          Look around you Stanly. Look at all the pain and
                 suffering your lie has caused.

                              STAN
     Well we only did it because Jimbo lied to us first.
     We had this report on the Vietnam War for school and
     we interviewed Jimbo about it. He made up all this
     stuff about Vietnam and he got us in trouble!!

                             JIMBO
             Hey now, everything that I told you
               about the war actually happened!

                              STAN
     Mr. Garrison said there was no way that you could
     have defeated the entire Viet Cong by yourself.

             The audience gets really silent.

                             JESUS
                 The ENTIRE Viet Cong army?

           Jimbo looks around nervously.

                             JIMBO
     I, uh... Well okay, I might have EMBELLISHED
       the truth a little, but that's different.

                             JESUS
                             Is it?

                             JIMBO
     Well sure, I mean... well no, I guess not.

                             JESUS
          And as for you Stan, I think you need
             to kick your drug habit and -

STAN
Wait a second, I don't take drugs! That was a lie!

JESUS
Wait, Jimbo made that up?

STAN
No, your producer did. She made Jimbo
tell everybody that I did drugs.

Jesus' smiles drops.

JESUS
What?!

STAN
During the break. Your producer came over and told Jimbo
what to say about me. She told him to lie!

JIMBO
It's true, she did. I'm such a tool.

JESUS
Oh really?

Jesus looks over at his producer who is
trying to hide behind a small plant.

KYLE
Yeah, then she told us to throw a chair at Ned!

CARTMAN
Yeah, I didn't want to do it Jesus! They made me do it!!

The crowd gets up and starts to bawl.

MAN IN THE CROWD
Screw this show! I thought this was all real!

The whole crowd walks out the door, right by Jesus.

JESUS
Wait everybody! Come back!

But they all leave. Jesus drops the mike.

BLACK MAN
Don't feel too bad Montel. We all want to touch
children sometimes, it's only natural...

COMMERCIAL BREAK - EPILOGUE

EXT. TELEVISION STUDIO

Jesus, Jimbo, Ned and the boys stand
outside the studio.

JIMBO
I'm sorry Stan, I was just trying to tell a good story.
I never meant for you boys to get in trouble.

STAN
We're sorry too Uncle Jimbo. We're sorry for making you
look stupid in front of the whole world.

KYLE
Yeah, and we're sorry for turning Ned into a vegetable.

JIMBO
Ah, he'll be fine. I'll just take him home
and show him some good hard-core porn and
he'll snap out of it. Won't you Ned?

Jimbo slaps Ned on the back. He falls over on his face.

Jesus walks in.

JESUS
I want to apologize to all of you for what happened in
there. In our competition for ratings we all lost sight
of why we got into show business in the first place.

JIMBO
Yeah, titties and beer.

JESUS
Actually I was referring more to the pursuit of truth
but... Well anyway, I can't wait to get back to my old
show without all the glitz and ratings and producers...

STAN
Wait a sec. Where IS your producer?

JESUS
I sent her away.

CARTMAN
Sent her away where?

INT. HELL - DAY

The producer is horrified as she walks around the flames
of hell with pitchforks stabbing her ass.

PRODUCER
WHAT IS THIS?! WHAT'S HAPPENING?!

SATAN
Welcome to my dominion.

PRODUCER
Aaaah...

The producer looks confused.

SADAM HUSSEIN
Eh, take a load off, put your feet up! Me and Satan were
just about to go shopping for furniture. Come on Satan.

SATAN
Okay honey.

They walk off hand in hand.

The producer looks up to the heavens.

PRODUCER
NOOOOOOOOOOOooooooooooo!!!

EPISODE 209
CHEF'S SALTY CHOCOLATE BALLS

BY TREY PARKER, MATT STONE & NANCY PIMENTHAL

EXT. UTAH - MOUNTAINS - DAY

A large banner strung across the street reads
'Sundance Film Festival!'

Hordes of Hollywood people line the streets.
Cars are everywhere, most of them honking their HORNS.
It's a mess.

The FILM CHAIRMAN, A Robert Redford type guy, and his
female assistant PHILLIS stand in the middle of the
chaos surveying it all.

FILM CHAIRMAN
Why do we hold the Sundance Film Festival here, Phillis?
It's so painfully crowded.

PHILLIS
Because people from LA love to come to a
quaint little mountain town for a few days,
and this gives them an excuse.

FILM CHAIRMAN
No, this used to be a quaint little mountain town.
Now look at it. Sushi restaurants, upscale clothes stores,
25 dollar parking, Liam Neeson... I tell you Phillis,
I think we've tapped this town's resources out.
We must move the festival to another small
mountain town and begin again.

PHILLIS
That's not a bad idea... But where?

EXT. SOUTH PARK - DAY

The quiet little mountain town looks very peaceful.

A few birds chirp. Everything is quiet and still.

A butterfly flutters through frame.

A lone South Park FLAGMAN walks over to the flag pole,
ties a flag to it and starts to raise it.

Squeak... Squeak... Squeak...

Finally the flag is raised, and with
a gust of wind, the flag quietly unfurls:
'1st Annual South Park Film Festival.'

Within seconds, an absolute WHIRLWIND of cars
and people flood the town.

The flagman stares in disbelief as South Park is
immediately and forcefully overcome with Hollywood types.

FLAGMAN
Whoa.

EXT. SOUTH PARK ELEMENTARY - DAY

Establishing.

INT. CLASSROOM - DAY

Mr. Garrison stands in front of the class
with his hand puppet, Mr. Twig.

                    MR. GARRISON
Okay, children, I have some very exciting news for you.
Why don't you tell them, Mr. Twig.

                    MR. TWIG
That's right, Mr. Garrison. The first annual South Park
Film Festival begins today!

The kids just sit there.

                    WENDY
Wow, cool!

                    KYLE
They're not gonna show that stupid ass
Godzilla movie again, are they?

                    MR. GARRISON
No, no, Kyle, these are INDEPENDENT films.

                    STAN
Like 'Independence Day?' That sucked ass too.

                    CARTMAN
No, dude, independent films are those
black and white hippie movies. They're always
about gay cowboys eating pudding.

                    WENDY
No they're not! Independent films are
produced outside the Hollywood system.
They're movies without all the glitz
and glamour of Hollywood.

                    CARTMAN
Yeah, you show me ONE independent film that ISN'T about
gay cowboys eating pudding!

                    WENDY
Once again you have NO IDEA what
you're talking about fat ass!

                    CARTMAN
I'm not fat, I just haven't grown into
my body yet, you skinny bitch.

                    MR. GARRISON
Eric, if you call Wendy a bitch one more time,
I'm sending you to the Principal's office.

CHEF'S SALTY CHOCOLATE BALLS

Eric looks really mad.

He just sits there and fumes for a little bit...

                    CARTMAN
                    Bitch.

Immediately, Cartman packs up his things.

                    MR. GARRISON
            That's it, Eric! You-

                    CARTMAN
                    I'm going!

Cartman walks out the door.

                    MR. GARRISON
        Anyway, children, I want you all to see at
        least ONE independent film at the festival
            and then write a paper about it.

            The kids moan.

                    MR. GARRISON
    The first film showing is called 'Witness to Denial' and
    is a sexual exploration piece about two women in love.

                    STAN
                    (To Kyle)
        Oh, my Uncle Jimbo has a ton of those
            movies in his dresser drawer.

EXT. SOUTH PARK STREET - DAY

Now there's also a big banner over the main street that
says '1st Annual South Park Film Festival!' Food tents
        and coffee stands line the sidewalks.

L.A. types are everywhere, cell phones to their ears,
    yapping away about this and that deal.

                HOLLYWOOD TYPE
    No, no, I want to shoot the script next month
            with Demi Moore attached...

            ANOTHER HOLLYWOOD TYPE
    Well you tell Spielberg he can kiss my ass!!

The Mayor and her assistant take it all in.

                    MAYOR
                    Wow...

South Park is absolutely overrun with people.
The Mayor and her assistant can barely move.

MAYOR
Look at this, Johnson. Traffic jams at every
intersection. Hoards of people pushing their way through
the crowds... It's almost like we're a real city!

The boys walk through the town, weaving their way
through the hordes of people.

CARTMAN
I can't believe I got sent to the Principal's office
because of your stupid girlfriend!

STAN
She's NOT my girlfriend!

KENNY
Mph rmphm rmph rm rmph.

Everyone laughs.

KYLE
Sick, Kenny!

STAN
Damn dude, look at all these people...

Just then a Hollywood type runs by
with a cell phone in hand.

HOLLYWOOD TYPE
I'm late for a screening. I'll call you from the theater!

KYLE
All this for a bunch of stupid movies?

The boys come across Chef, who is setting up a booth.
His makeshift sign reads 'Chef's Soul Food.'

CHEF
Hello there, children!

BOYS
Hey, Chef.

STAN
Whatchya doing?

CHEF
Children, this whole film festival thing has
quite lucrative monetary possibilities. Now I'm gonna
sell some of my famous cookies to these Hollywood
types and make a MINT!

CARTMAN
What kind of cookies?

KYLE
Calm down, tubby.

CHEF'S SALTY CHOCOLATE BALLS

CHEF
They're little cookies with fudge in the middle.
And I call them 'Fudge 'ems.'

Chef holds up a colorful box that has
'Chef's FUDGE 'EMS' on the front.

CARTMAN
I wanna fudge 'em.

CHEF
(Daydreaming)
I can just see the commercial now...
'Wife got you down? Boss making you angry?
Kids yelling at you?
(Holding up the box)
Well... FUDGE 'EM!'

KYLE
Cool!

CHEF
And I've also got my double-chocolate cookies 'Fudge This.'

A few executives walk by.

HOLLYWOOD TYPE
Oh look, one of the natives is selling
local food wares! How quaint.

FEMALE HOLLYWOOD TYPE
This is why I come to these things. To get away from L.A.
and become one with a more simple culture.

CHEF
Well, perhaps you'd like to try my low calorie cookies-
(Holding up box)
'Go Fudge Yourself'. Or my all natural-
(Holding up box)
'I Don't Really Give a Flying Fudge.'

FEMALE HOLLYWOOD TYPE
Ooh... Do you have any tofu or steamed celery?

CHEF
Huh?

HOLLYWOOD TYPE
I would kill for some cous cous right now.

CHEF
Who's cous?

FEMALE HOLLYWOOD TYPE
Uh... Never mind. We brought some food
from the natural market in L.A.

HOLLYWOOD TYPE
Cute sign though.

They walk off.

Wendy walks up to Stan.

WENDY
Stan, I have two tickets for the opening film of the
festival. Would you still like to come with me?

CARTMAN
(Mimicking her)
Maa, Ma ma ma mama ma ma mamama ma ma
ma mamama. Ma ma ma ma ma ma ma?

STAN
Shut up, Cartman.
(To Wendy)
Sure, dude. I mean, since we have to
write a paper on a film anyway.

Stan and Wendy walk away happily.

CARTMAN
She'll be the death of him, Kyle.
Mark my words, she'll be the death of him.

Kyle looks at Cartman quizzically.

KYLE
If she holds his hand in that theater it'll be all over...

CHEF
(Calling)
Get 'em while they're hot. My all new cookies:
'I just went and Fudged your Momma.'

CARTMAN
Jesus, he sure ran that one into the ground.

EXT. MOVIE THEATER - NIGHT

Wendy and Stan walk up to the South Park Theater,
where scores of people wait to get in.

The marquee reads, 'Witness to Denial.'

INT. MOVIE THEATER - NIGHT

Stan and Wendy are seated in the front row.
They are surrounded by industry people.

Stan is munching on popcorn and sipping on a coke.

STAN
When's this thing start?
I hope there's some good previews.

CHEF'S SALTY CHOCOLATE BALLS

                    WENDY
        Stan, film festival movies don't
        usually have previews before them.

                    STAN
                 THEY WHAT?!?!

ON THE MOVIE SCREEN:

        A title comes up that reads 'Witness to Denial.'
        Then 'A sexual exploration piece by Candice Butch.'

                A few people applaud.

        The film is in black and white and the scene
              is very serious and dramatic.

                   WOMAN #1
        Who are you to judge my womanly soul?
        The Goddess flames that burn in my memory aren't dark.
               Dare you call them dark.

                   WOMAN #1
           Here lies the truth of my body.

                    STAN
                  Oh, brother.

                 WOMAN #1 (cont'd)
        The goddess that cries - FREEDOM!
        Here is Goddess truth of my womanly being!

ANGLE - STAN

              He looks down at Wendy's hand.
        She picks it up, moves it over his as if she's
        going to take it, then just sets it down again.
              Stan breaths a sigh of relief.

ANGLE - SCREEN

                   WOMAN #2
        You are my blossom. My flame. When we make love, it's like
               the sun is right outside the door.

                   WOMAN #1
           Then make love to me right now...

              They fall to the floor.

ANGLE BACK ON WENDY AND STAN:

        Wendy is crying. Stan sits with his mouth agape.

                    STAN
                    Dude!

WENDY
Shhh!

STAN
Dude!

EXT. KYLE'S HOUSE - NIGHT

Establishing.

INT. KYLE'S HOUSE - NIGHT

Kyle is in the bathroom, sitting on the toilet going
poopies and singing softly.

KYLE
I can see clearly now, the rain is gone...
I can see all obstacles in my way...

KYLE'S MOTHER (O.S.)
Boobala, you need to get bed it's late.

KYLE
I'm poopies, ma!

KYLE'S MOTHER (O.S.)
Well, hurry it up.

KYLE
Gone are the dark clouds that had me-

VOICE
Kyyyyllleee...

Kyle stops singing and looks around quizzically.
Again the voice comes, it sounds week and needy.

VOICE
Kyyyyyyllllleeeeee...

KYLE
Could it be?

VOICE
Hoowwwddyy hooooooo...

KYLE
Mr. Hankey?!

Kyle jumps off the toilet and
sticks his head in the bowl.

KYLE
Mr. Hankey, is that you?

No answer.

KYLE
Hello?

Kyle reaches down and splashes the water around.

KYLE
Hello?!

EXT. SOUTH PARK - DAY

Establishing. The sun rises.

EXT. AVENUE DE LOS MEXICANOS - DAY

It appears that South Park is even more crowded
now than before.

A NEWSCASTER is amidst the hustle and bustle.

NEWSCASTER
I'm here live in South Park, Colorado where citizens of
Los Angeles are arriving in droves for the town's
First Annual Film Festival.

FOOTAGE shows traffic jams, trash cans overfilled and a
VERY LONG line for the bathroom.

NEWSCASTER (cont'd)
This is just a small, quiet mountain community
where nothing out of the ordinary ever really
happens, (except for the occasional complete
destruction of the entire town) and so the
excitement level is naturally very high.
Right now, the townspeople are anxiously awaiting the
arrival of some of Hollywood's top celebrities.

The boys are standing across the street, along with
several townspeople, waiting to see something.

KYLE
It was him, dude, I tell you it was Mr. Hankey.

CARTMAN
Wait, I thought Mr. Hankey only came at Christmas time.

KYLE
Well I'm SURE it was him.

(MOVED)

TOWNSPERSON
LOOK!! LOOK!! HERE COMES SOMEBODY!!!

Everyone frantically tries to get a look, as a large
limousine pulls up in front of the theater.

The door opens, everyone holds their breath.
From the car emerges FRED SAVAGE.

He is wearing a T-shirt that says 'I'm Fred Savage!'

ANNOUNCER
Ladies and Gentlemen, T.V.'s Fred Savage!!

TOWNSPEOPLE
(Disappointed)
Aw!!

Fred Savage puts his head down and
walks sheepishly into the theater.

TOWNSPERSON
Well, I'm sure a real person will show up soon.

KYLE
So how was that movie last night, dude?

STAN
Oh, dude, you don't even want to know.

CARTMAN
It had a bunch of gay cowboys eating pudding, huh!

Stan thinks.

STAN
Yeah, pretty much.

CARTMAN
Yeah.

STAN
That theater sucks, though,
they need to get a bigger screen.

KYLE
They should project the movies on Cartman's ass.

The boys laugh.

CARTMAN
HEY!

STAN
Yeah, but that'd be like IMAX!

They laugh more.

CARTMAN
Okay, that's enough fat ass jokes for this week.

KENNY
(Telling a fat ass joke)
Mph rmph rmphm rmphmh rmpmh, rmpmh rmpmh rmphmh.

The boys laugh REALLY hard.

CARTMAN
Okay, that does it! Screw you guys I'm going home!!

Cartman just sits there and waits.

And waits.

KYLE
Well?

CARTMAN
I'm GONNA, just give me a minute.

The film chairman and his assistant are watching the
chaos that has consumed the South Park streets.

FILM CHAIRMAN
This is perfect. Why didn't we think of it sooner.
This town still has some charm left, not the
mess we turned Park City into.

PHILLIS
Forgive me for being observant, but...
Won't we just end up doing the same thing to THIS town?

The chairman thinks.

FILM CHAIRMAN
Yes... And the town after, and the town after that. Like
termites we will move this film festival from town to
town until we have used it up, and then move on, until
every quiet mountain town is like Los Angeles.

PHILLIS
Why? Why would we do such a thing?

FILM CHAIRMAN
Because WE have to live in L.A., and if we can't
live in a quiet, simple peaceful mountain town...
Then NOBODY will!!

The film chairman laughs maniacally.

FILM CHAIRMAN (cont'd)
Wait, wait, wait. Zoom in to a close-up
on my face when I do that! Ready?

The film chairman laughs again.
This time the camera ZOOMS IN on his face.

FILM CHAIRMAN (cont'd)
Then nobody will... That's it.

ANGLE - BOYS

As they walk in front of Chef's food stand.

Chef actually appears to be happy again. His sign that
said 'Chef's Soul Food' now says 'Chef's Salty Balls.'

                          BOYS
                       Hey, Chef.

                          CHEF
         Children! I'm glad you're here! I want you to
       check out my new confectioneries! I think they're
        gonna sell right through the roof! I call them
            'Chef's Salty Chocolate Balls.'

              The boys look at each other.

                          STAN
                    Are they good?

                          CHEF
                       Try em!

           The boys all take one and eat them.

                          STAN
                 Hey, these are good!

                        CARTMAN
        Yeah, I love your salty chocolate balls Chef.

                   Kenny laughs.

ANGLE - ON A SEWER DRAIN

           We hear the voice of Mr. Hankey.

                          VOICE
                 Kyyyylllleeee...

                          KYLE
                      (Snapping)
                  There it is again!

                          STAN
                There's what again?

                          VOICE
                 Kyyylllleeee...

         Kyle turns his head in the direction of the voice.

         From KYLE'S POV we see a sewer grill.

                          KYLE
       It's Mr. Hankey! I think he's in some kind of trouble.

                          STAN
       Dude, how do you tell if a piece of poo is in trouble?

CHEF'S SALTY CHOCOLATE BALLS

KYLE
Where does that grill go?

STAN
To the sewer dude.

KYLE
Of course! The SEWER!! That must be where he is!! COME ON!!

Kyle dashes off. The other boys just stand there.

After a few beats, Kyle pops in again.

KYLE
Come ON!

Chef is at his stand and breaks
into song to attract customers.

CHEF
Say everybody have you seen my balls?
They're big and salty and brown.
If you ever need a quick pick-me-up
just stick my balls in your mouth.
Ooh, suck on my chocolate salty balls,
put 'em in your mouth and suck 'em and suck 'em.

FIRST COMMERCIAL BREAK

INT. SEWER - DAY

The boys walk through the dark, creepy sewer.
Kyle and Stan have flashlights.

CARTMAN
Oh man, it smells like ass down here!

KYLE
Of course it smells like ass, retard!
It's a sewer!

Suddenly, there is an ECHOING RATTLE.

STAN
WHAT WAS THAT?!

Stan spins around and shines his flashlight
on a small rat. It scurries off.

CARTMAN
Oh man, let's get outta here!

KYLE
We can't dude, not until we find Mr. Hankey!

Now a HUGE BOOMING SOUND causes the boys to turn around.

Kyle shines his flashlight on a shadowed creature!!

SOUTH PARK

Scene 139	Panel	BG

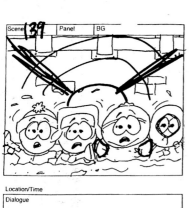

Location/Time

Dialogue

BOYS
AAAAAGGHGH!!

Action/Efx

Trans.

21

Scene 140B	Panel	BG S/A 138

Location/Time

Dialogue

Garrison steps into the light

Action/Efx

The creature steps into a shaft of light. It isn't a monster
at all, but rather a man in a SCUBA outfit.

Trans.

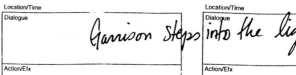

Scene 140 Cont'd	Panel	BG

Location/Time

Dialogue

Action/Efx

Trans.

26

SOUTH PARK

Scene 141	Panel	BG

Location/Time

Dialogue

KYLE
What the hell?

Action/Efx

Trans.

14

Scene 142	Panel	BG

Location/Time

Dialogue

Action/Efx

The man takes off his snorkel and mask
revealing that he is Mr. Garrison.

Trans.

22

Scene 143	Panel	BG

Location/Time

Dialogue

STAN
Mr. Garrison?

Action/Efx

Trans.

18

It has its arms out.

                    BOYS
                AAAAAGGHGH!!

The creature steps into a shaft of light. It isn't a
monster at all, but rather a man in a SCUBA outfit.

                    KYLE
                What the hell?

The man takes off his snorkel and mask
revealing that he is Mr. Garrison.

                    STAN
                Mr. Garrison?

                MR. GARRISON
            Oh, uh... Hello children...

                  CARTMAN
      What are you doing down in the sewer
         with a bunch of snorkel stuff on?

                MR. GARRISON
        Oh... I... I was just... a... Hanging out.

                    KYLE
                In a sewer?

                MR. GARRISON
    Children, do you know how to file a police report?

                    BOYS
                    No.

                MR. GARRISON
            Good. See you in school.

With that, Garrison dashes away.
The boys look at each other.

INT. DEEPER IN THE SEWER - DAY

The boys are still walking onward
through the catacombs of the sewer.

                  CARTMAN
    This is ridiculous. What the hell are we, the Goonies?

                    KYLE
        Yeah, we're the Goonies, Cartman.
    Why don't you pretend like you're the fat kid.

                  CARTMAN
    Okay, that does it. Screw you guys, I'm home.

SOUTH PARK

Scene 155	Panel	BG

Location/Time

Dialogue

CARTMAN
Okay, that does it. Screw you guys, I'm going home.

Action/Efx

Trans.

85

Scene 156	Panel	BG

Location/Time

Dialogue

MR. HANKEY (o.s.)
(Hoooowddyy HO!!!!!!)

Action/Efx

Trans.

→

Scene 156 Cont'd.	Panel	BG

Location/Time

Dialogue

Mr. Hankey (cont'd)(o.s.)
(Hooowddyy Ho!!!)

Action/Efx

The boys all spin around...

Trans.

21

Do the Hankey Hand wave.

SOUTH PARK

Scene 157	Panel	BG

Location/Time

Dialogue

Mr. Hankey (cont'd)
Howwwddyy Ho!!!

Action/Efx
Arl New Setup Since TD had

to see Mr. Hankey! He is in a little row boat, wearing a sailor's cap.

Trans.
No Santa Cap. but instead his sailor cap

43

Scene 158	Panel	BG

Location/Time

Dialogue

KYLE
MR. HANKEY!!

Action/Efx
boards (see Eric)

Trans.

22

Scene 159	Panel	BG

Location/Time

Dialogue

MR. HANKEY
Howdy Ho, boys!!

KYLE
I told you guys he'd be here!!

(looking at other)

Action/Efx
Mr Hankey floats into frame

Trans.

70

MR. HANKEY
Hooooowddyyy HO!!!!!!

The boys all spin around to see Mr. Hankey!
He is in a little row boat, wearing a sailor's cap.

KYLE
MR. HANKEY!!

MR. HANKEY
Howdy Ho, boys!!

KYLE
I told you guys he'd be here!!

MR. HANKEY
Gosh look at ya! You're all growing up so fast!

CARTMAN
(Put off)
Hi Mr. Hankey, nice to see you.

MR. HANKEY
Have you all been brushing behind your teeth?

BOYS
Yes.

MR. HANKEY
And using dental floss?

BOYS
Yes.

MR. HANKEY
And washing behind your ears?

BOYS
Yes.

CARTMAN
...No.

Mr. Hankey coughs.

KYLE
What's the matter, Mr. Hankey? Are you sick?

MR. HANKEY
Oh, I've just got a little cold is all. All these new
people in South Park are stressful on my home.

STAN
What do you mean?

MR. HANKEY
Well, you see boys, the sewer is a fragile ecosystem.

CARTMAN
(Rolling his eyes)
Oh my God...

MR. HANKEY
These new folks in town eat nothing but cous cous, tofu
and raw vegetables, and it's destroying my environment.

KYLE
And that's why you've got a cold?

MR. HANKEY
That's why, Kyle... That's why.

STAN
Well why don't you ask them to leave?

MR. HANKEY
There's only one time a year I can come to the
surface and that's Christmas time. That's why
I need you boys to go for me.

Mr. Hankey starts coughing again.

KYLE
Don't worry Mr. Hankey, we'll go
tell everyone!! Come on, guys!!

The boys dash off.

MR. HANKEY
Don't forget to change your sheets once a week!

EXT. SOUTH PARK - DAY

The streets are jammed solid.
People are all over the place.

EXT. MOVIE THEATER - DAY

Establishing. The marquee reads,
'A BUNCH OF GAY COWBOYS EATING PUDDING.'

INT. MOVIE THEATER - DAY

The theater is packed with Hollywood types,
all whom have cell phones. A wiry FILMMAKER
stands in front of the screen.

FILMMAKER
So, without further ado, we will begin this amazing film.
It is a work of blood sweat and tears...

Just then, Kyle and the boys come dashing in.

KYLE
Wait! Stop!

The crowd starts to buzz.

KYLE
Could I have your attention, please?

MAN IN CROWD
Is that Leonardo DiCaprio?

Suddenly tons of flashes go off in Kyle's face.

KYLE
AAAGH!!

ANOTHER MAN
No, no wait, that's not him.

Just as suddenly, the flashes stop.

KYLE
Ladies and gentlemen, my best friend, Mr. Hankey,
is getting sick because South Park has become
overcrowded with people who eat health food.

The crowd murmurs.

LADY IN CROWD
Excuse me little boy... What's a Mr. Hankey?

KYLE
He's a talking piece of poo that lives in the sewer.
But now he's getting sick because his eggosystem is all
out of whack because of all the extra poo in the sewer.
If you don't all leave and go home soon, Mr. Hankey's
gonna die... He's one of my best friends in the whole
wide world and I don't want him to die.

Kyle hangs his head. The crowd takes in the sight of
this lonely child standing on stage.

A beat.

HOLLYWOOD TYPE
What a great story!! It has everything!!

FEMALE HOLLYWOOD TYPE
This could be the next Free Willy!

HOLLYWOOD TYPE
Great pitch, son! How much do you want for it?!

KYLE
Huh?

Now a development guy stands up.

DEVELOPMENT GUY
Does it have to be a talking piece of poo?

The boys look at each other.

                    HOLLYWOOD TYPE
It be a crime-fighting rabbit. Or a lovable turtle!

                    HOLLYWOOD TYPE #1
This could be a great summer movie!

                    HOLLYWOOD TYPE #2
Can we put a monkey in it?

                    HOLLYWOOD TYPE #3
'The Mr. Hankey Story!' Is Harrison Ford
available for a fall pic?

                    HOLLYWOOD TYPE #1
Keanu Reeves.

                    HOLLYWOOD TYPE #2
Matt Damon!

                    FRED SAVAGE
Fred Savage!

Fred is sitting there in his 'I'm Fred Savage!' T-Shirt.

Everyone now goes silent with shock for a beat, and then
laughs a little. Fred looks put off.

                    HOLLYWOOD TYPE #1
I'll pay a million for this story!

                    HOLLYWOOD TYPE #3
I'll pay two!

The place absolutely ERUPTS as the bidding continues.

            Kyle sadly walks off the stage past Stan,
            Cartman and Kenny.

                    KYLE
Dude, no one even listened to me.

                    STAN
You know, it does sound like a pretty sweet movie.

A Hollywood type walks up and takes Cartman aside.

        *NOTE - redo this dialogue WHISPERING.

                    HOLLYWOOD TYPE
I take it you're part owner of this
whole Mr. Hooey story, right?

                    CARTMAN
Huh, uh, yeah I guess.

HOLLYWOOD TYPE
I want you to do a big money deal with me.

CARTMAN
All of us?

HOLLYWOOD TYPE
Well... I can see that you're the real brains of the
group. You don't really need those guys do you?

Cartman looks at his friends.

CARTMAN
Yeah, screw those guys. I don't even like them.

HOLLYWOOD TYPE
That's great, kid. Let's make a deal.

EXT. SOUTH PARK STREET - LIBRARY - DAY

The Hollywood types are scurrying around like ants.
There seems to be even more of them than before.

The Film chairman and his assistant stand in front
of a small, quaint library.

FILM CHAIRMAN
Ladies and gentlemen I want to thank you all for making
the First Annual South Park Film Festival a success.
We've barely even started and already the festival has
seen more attendance than last year's Sundance Festival!

The Hollywood type cheer.

FILM CHAIRMAN (cont'd)
And I am VERY pleased to announce, that in honor of the
South Park people who have welcomed us, we are going to
build a HOLLYWOOD PLANET restaurant right here where
this library used to stand!

Suddenly, a huge demolition block swings in
and knocks down the library.

The South Park people gasp.
Everyone looks concerned, even the Mayor.

MAYOR'S ASSISTANT
Can they do that?

MAYOR
They're Hollywood, they can do anything.

INT. SEWER - DAY

Kyle, alone, is wandering through
the sewer with his flashlight.

                         KYLE
                    (Calling out)
                    Mr. Hankey?

          Kyle's voice echoes through the sewer,
                 but there is no reply.

          Kyle's sighs, but then hears strange
             ORGAN MUSIC in the distance.

       Kyle turns and heads toward the source of the music.

                INT. SEWER CHAMBER - DAY

          Kyle enters a different little area, which is lit
                brighter from a grill up above.

          Kyle looks around the room, and his eyes finally
          fall upon Mr. Hankey, who has his back to Kyle,
                and is playing a HUGE pipe organ.

             Now we see Mr. Hankey from the front,
                he is intense on his playing.

                         KYLE
                    Mr. Hankey?

          Finally, Kyle interrupts him.

                         KYLE
                    Mr. Hankey?

          Mr. Hankey stops playing and turns around.

                      MR. HANKEY
          Oh, Kyle, Howdy Ho! (cough, cough, cough)

          Kyle walks up to Mr. Hankey's side.

                      MR. HANKEY
          Well? How did it go? Is everyone gonna
             stop poopin' in my environment?

             Kyle hangs his head.

                         KYLE
       They didn't believe me. They thought I was pitching a movie.

                      MR. HANKEY
                    Oh... I see...

       Mr. Hankey looks really sad as he coughs some more.

                   MR. HANKEY (cont'd)
       Well, shucks, Kyle. I can't thank you enough for trying.

                         KYLE
       We only have one option. I've got to take you to the surface!

MR. HANKEY
I can't. The sun'll dry me out.

KYLE
It's the only way to prove to them that you're real.

MR. HANKEY
But I won't last long up above.

KYLE
Well you're not gonna last down here either, Mr. Hankey.
Now come on, I'm not gonna let you die!!

MR. HANKEY
Alright, just let me get my toothbrush.

EXT. MOVIE THEATER - DAY

Stan and Wendy walk up to the theater.

WENDY
Come on, Stan! We're gonna be late for the screening.

Stan and Wendy look up at the marquee.
It reads 'Tom Hanks in: ME & Mr. HANKEY.'

STAN
Geez, they made that into a movie already?

INT. MOVIE THEATER - DAY

Stan and Wendy sit in the packed theater.
Stan looks bored as usual.

ON THE MOVIE SCREEN:

Tom Hanks lies in a hospital bed dying.

TOM HANKS
Mr. Hankey, I can't go on anymore. I've lost the fight.

CHIMPANZEE
No, I'm not leaving without you. We started this together
and we're gonna finish it together.

And with that, the chimp grabs Tom Hanks' hand.

TOM HANKS
I always thought death was something
glorious but now I know that it's not.

ANGLE ON WENDY AND STAN:

Wendy is crying her eyes out with a tissue. Stan looks
at Wendy, and then places his hand out carefully in
front of her. Not on her seat, but enough
to maybe get the signal across.

Wendy blows her nose, and Stan raises his hand
a little, trying to catch Wendy's eye.

She does, and places the wet tissue in
Stan's open hand. Stan frowns.

ANGLE - BACK OF THE THEATER

Meanwhile, the Hollywood type is watching the film with
Cartman, who is still wearing sunglasses.

> HOLLYWOOD TYPE
> It's going over really well. People are gonna
> be knocking my door down to get you.

> CARTMAN
> WHO THE HELL CAST TOM HANKS IN THIS?!
> TOM HANKS CAN'T ACT HIS WAY OUT OF A NUTSACK!

ANGLE - SCREEN

> TOM HANKS
> I'll always love you, Mr. Hankey...

> CARTMAN
> (Mimicking him)
> MA MAMA MA MA, MAMA MAMA.

EXT. MOVIE THEATER - DAY

Kenny is standing outside of the theater playing with
his yo-yo. Just then the huge crowd is let out of the
movie and he gets trampled to death.

> MAN #1
> Oh my God, I found a penny.

> MAN #2
> You bastard!

EXT. STREET - DAY

A sewer grill pops up from the street, and Kyle emerges
carrying a little box.

> KYLE
> Okay, Mr. Hankey, we're out. How are you doing?

Mr. Hankey is covered with white cloth
and wearing little sunglasses. He looks just
like Brando in 'Island of Dr. Moreau.'

> MR. HANKEY
> It sure is dry up here. (cough, cough)

> KYLE
> Don't worry, we'll do this quick okay?
> Just hang on, Mr. Hankey, just hang on!

CHEF'S SALTY CHOCOLATE BALLS

COMMERCIAL BREAK

EXT. PLANET HOLLYWOOD - DAY

The huge, towering, bright building
is already taking shape.

The film chairman, wearing a hardhat,
surveys his masterpiece.

The Mayor, also wearing a hardhat,
walks up with her assistants.

MAYOR
Excuse me, Mr. Film Commissioner,
could I have a word with you?

FILM CHAIRMAN
Make it quick.

MAYOR
Well, the people of my town are a little upset.
I don't think we realized what an impact this
festival would have on our town.

FILM CHAIRMAN
Uh-huh.

MAYOR
Right, so we were actually wondering
if we could call this whole thing off.

FILM CHAIRMAN
(Still looking at building)
We have contracts. You try to pull out now, and we'll sue
your little town for every penny it's got.

As the chairman says this, he holds
contracts in front of the Mayor's face.

FILM CHAIRMAN
But thanks so much for the hard work!

Across the street, Stan and Chef stand among the unhappy
South Parkians watching the giant mess go up.

Meanwhile, Cartman is standing
off to the side with his Hollywood type.

CARTMAN
But this doesn't make sense Marty!
You told me the movie made a lot of money!

HOLLYWOOD TYPE
Right, two million, minus your agent's fee, minus your
lawyer's fee minus my fee and with publicity and taxes
taken out, you get three dollars. That's more than most
people in your position make, trust me.

Stan walks up to Cartman as the
Hollywood type moves away.

STAN
Serves you right Cartman! You're a sellout!!

CARTMAN
I am not a sellout!! What's a sellout?!

STAN
If you work in the entertainment business and
you make money you're a sellout!

Now Chef walks up and sits on the curb.

CHEF
It's all gone to hell, children. And we're all to blame...

Chef glances over at his food stand.

CHEF
Even me. I was selling out my town too.
And now look at it.

STAN
So what do we do now?

CHEF
There's nothing we can do.
Just sit here and suck on my balls.

Chef pours some of the candy
into Stan and Cartman's hands.

Just then, Kyle comes running up.

KYLE
YOU GUYS!!! WE HAVE TO HURRY!!

STAN
Why?

KYLE
Come on! Everything's gonna be okay!

Stan, Cartman and Chef follow Kyle
as he runs up to the film chairman.

KYLE
Sir... Sir!

FILM CHAIRMAN
Not now.

KYLE
I have to show you something. I think it will change
the way you feel about your impact here.

CHEF'S SALTY CHOCOLATE BALLS

Phillis and a few other Hollywood types gather around.

                    HOLLYWOOD TYPE
                    What's this?

                         KYLE
        I want you guys to all meet my friend.

Kyle opens the box and holds it out.

        After a few seconds, a cold, white
        lump of shit falls to the ground.

        Kyle looks at it, horrified.

Stan and Cartman look horrified as well.

The Hollywood types just look extremely unimpressed.

                    FILM CHAIRMAN
    That's great kid. A dried out lump of shit. Very compelling.
                    (Calling out)
    Okay folks! Let's move! We gotta have that sign done in
                time for the opening tonight!

Everyone walks away. Kyle kneels down to Mr. Hankey,
        Chef puts a hand on Kyle's shoulder.

                         KYLE
        You can't die, Mr. Hankey... You can't.

                      MR. HANKEY
        Kyle... before I go, there is something
        I must tell you. Come closer...

Kyle moves in a little.

                   MR. HANKEY (cont'd)
                    Closer...

Kyle moves in more.

                         KYLE
        Well, what is it, Mr. Hankey?

                      MR. HANKEY
        There is another Skywalker.

And with that, Mr. Hankey lets out a final breath and dies.

                         KYLE
                    Noooooooo!

                      MR. HANKEY
                    Wait Kyle.

                         KYLE
        What is it Mr. Hankey?

> MR. HANKEY
> Come closer.

> KYLE
> What is it?

> MR. HANKEY
> Closer...

> KYLE
> Yes?

> MR. HANKEY
> Closer! One time, when you were sleeping, I put myself
> in your mouth and had my friend take a picture.

And with that, Mr. Hankey dies again.

Kyle bursts into tears.

> KYLE
> Nooo!!

Roll montage of Mr. Hankey from Christmas
episode in happier times. Mr. Hankey song
sung slowly à la Jimmy Durante.

Out of nowhere, a GOVERNMENT WORKER
wearing a white containment suit walks up.

> GOVERNMENT WORKER
> I'm sorry, son. Let's get him to ICU.

The Government worker zips up Mr. Hankey
in a little plastic body bag.

> KYLE
> No. No!!!!

> STAN
> Are you gonna be okay, dude? I'm here for you.

Just then Wendy walks up.

> WENDY
> Hi, Stan. Ready to go see another movie?

> STAN
> Okay!

Stan and Wendy skip away.

EXT. MOVIE THEATER - DAY

Now the marquee reads 'Bow down to Hollywood
South Park' - and then in smaller letters below it:
'A film by Tom M. Pooner.'

CHEF'S SALTY CHOCOLATE BALLS

INT. MOVIE THEATER - DAY

Again Stan and Wendy are sitting down,
watching the movie. As it plays, Stan again
puts his hand out to be held.

Wendy looks down at Stan's hand and then looks at him.
Stan immediately pulls his hand away and then
goes back to watching the movie.

ANGLE - SCREEN

Two cowboys are eating pudding.

COWBOY #1
Say, Tom, do have any pudding left?

COWBOY #2
I ate all mine up, silly.

COWBOY #1
Well then, now what do we do?

ANGLE - STAN and WENDY

Stan again gingerly puts out his hand.
Wendy looks down at it. Stan again pulls it away.

But this time, Wendy reaches over, takes Stan's hand, and
holds in hers. She smiles at him. Stan smiles, and then
vomits on the person in front of him.

WENDY
Ew!

AUDIENCE MEMBER
Hey!

STAN
Sorry.

ANGLE - SCREEN

COWBOY #1
Well, why don't we just explore our sexuality.

COWBOY #2
Oh, good idea. Let's.

They move in close to each other.

ANGLE - STAN and WENDY

Stan's eyes grow wide.

STAN
Oh dude! I shouldn't be seeing this!

SOUTH PARK

PROD. # _____
SC. 32 01
Scene 333 | Panel | BG

PAGE 142

SC.
Scene 334 | Panel | BG

SC.
Scene 335 | Panel | BG

Location/Time INT. HOSPITIAL - NIGHT

Animator Change pol.

Dialogue

Action/Efx
Kyle is in a hospital with white
containment plastic everywhere (think E.T.).

Trans.

22

Location/Time

Dialogue

Action/Efx

Little Mr. Hankey is lying dead on a
white bed with some   small flowers around him.

Trans.

21

Location/Time

Dialogue
        KYLE
        (Sobbing)
I'll never forget you. You were my best
friend after Stan.

Action/Efx

Trans.

78

PROD. # _____
SC.
Scene 336-01 | BG

SOUTH PARK

PAGE 143 B

SC.
Scene 336-02 | BG

SC.
Scene 336-02 cont

Location/Time

Dialogue
        KYLE
Chef... Does poo go to heaven?

Action/Efx
have Kyle turn
to look up at Chef.

Trans.

40

Location/Time

Dialogue
        CHEF
Uhh... Well, I

Action/Efx

Chef has to think long and hard.

Trans.

Location/Time

Dialogue
        Chef (cont'd)
    kind of hope not...

Action/Efx

Trans.

67

CHEF'S SALTY CHOCOLATE BALLS

Stan again vomits on the guy in front of him.

                    AUDIENCE MEMBER
          Is there a problem, young man?!

                         STAN
               No problem, dude.

EXT. HOSPITAL - NIGHT

               Establishing.

INT. HOSPITAL - NIGHT

Kyle and Chef in a hospital with white containment
          plastic everywhere (think ET).

Little Mr. Hankey is lying dead on a white bed with
          some small flowers around him.

                         KYLE
                       (Sobbing)
     I'll never forget you. You were my best friend after Stan.

                         CHEF
          Come on, Kyle, it's time to go.

                         KYLE
          Chef... Does poo go to heaven?

Chef has to think long and hard.

                         CHEF
               Well, I kind of hope not...

Kyle starts CRYING again.

                         CHEF
               I mean, sure it does...

Chef pulls out a chocolate from his pocket.

                         CHEF
          Here, I'll give him one my salty balls
               to take with him to poo heaven.

Chef puts the ball in Mr. Hankey's mouth.

                         CHEF
               Come on let's go...

Chef and Kyle get up and head out.

                    MR. HANKEY
               Kyyyllleeee...

Kyle spins around.

PROD. # _____
SC.

Scene 336-06 Panel Cel   BG S/A 333

Location/Time

Dialogue

           CHEF
     Come on let's go...

Action/Efx

Trans.

7

SOUTH PARK

SC.
cont.
336-06 cont.

Location/Time

Dialogue

Action/Efx

     Chef and Kyle get up and head out.

Trans.

62

SC.   PAGE 143 E

Scene 336-07   BG S/A 336.05

Location/Time

Dialogue

           MR. HANKEY
     Kyyyllleeee...

Action/Efx

try in betweens
on eye lids

Trans.

48

PROD. # _____
SC.

Scene 336-08 Panel BG

Location/Time

Dialogue

           KYLE
     Mr. Hankey?!

Action/Efx

     Kyle spins around.

Trans.

22

SC.

Scene 336-09 Panel BG S/A 334

Location/Time

Dialogue

     Mr. Hanky
     Kyyyylllleee...

Action/Efx

Trans.

69

SC.   PAGE 143 F

Scene 336-10 BG 333

Location/Time

Dialogue

           KYLE
     He's back!! He's back!!

Action/Efx

Trans.

38

KYLE
Mr. Hankey?!

MR. HANKEY
Howwwdy... Hooooo...

KYLE
He's back!! He's back!!

MR. HANKEY
That was delicious!

CHEF
My salty chocolate balls must have rejuvenated him!!

KYLE
You've got the best balls in the whole world, Chef!!

CHEF
You're damn right!

COMMERCIAL BREAK

EXT. PLANET HOLLYWOOD - DAY

A gala celebration has started out front of Planet
Hollywood. A banner reads 'GRAND OPENING!'
Balloons and decorations are everywhere.

Cartman has opened a little stand, where he
appears to be selling something.

CARTMAN
STEP ON UP, GET THEM HERE!! MR. HANKEY AND ME T-SHIRTS!!

Cartman holds out the T-shirts with a
picture of Tom Hanks and the Monkey.

CARTMAN
GET THEM WHILE THEY LAST FOLKS!! ONLY $14.95!!

HOLLYWOOD TYPE
I'll take two.

The Hollywood types are coming in droves handing
Cartman money and taking the T-shirts.

CARTMAN
Selling T-shirts kicks ass.

Meanwhile, the film chairman takes his place at
a podium with a microphone.

FILM CHAIRMAN
Ladies and gentlemen, I am pleased to announce, on this
gala opening of Planet Hollywood South Park, that the
festival will be back next year, and the year after that,
and the year after that, and so on!

The Hollywood people cheer. The South Park people moan.

                    FILM CHAIRMAN (cont'd)
                And now... Release the curtain!!

        The curtain drops, and the GIGANTIC Planet
        Hollywood sign is revealed. It spins around
                slowly with flashing lights.

                    FILM CHAIRMAN (cont'd)
                I give you Hollywood in South Park!!

        The South Parkians gasp at the size of the sign.

                            KYLE
                           WAIT!!!

        Kyle, Cartman and Stan come running up behind everybody
            holding little Mr. Hankey. Everyone turns around.

                            KYLE
            I brought him! I brought him to show you!!

                        FILM CHAIRMAN
                      Oh not this again.

                            KYLE
                     Behold Mr. Hankey!

        Mr. Hankey jumps out of his little basket magically.

                        MR. HANKEY
                  HOOOOOWWWWDDDY HO!!

        The Hollywood people just stare at it for a while,
                    and then turn back around.

                        FILM CHAIRMAN
            Anyway, this new Planet Hollywood will be the
                official meeting place for all...

                        MR. HANKEY
        Howdy Ho, folks! It sure is nice to see you all. But I'm
        afraid my buddy Kyle was right, there's not enough
        room in South Park to accommodate a festival.

                        HOLLYWOOD TYPE
        Mr. Poo, if you wouldn't mind, we can't hear our chairman.
        If you could just turn yourself down, you're at about a
        seven right now and we need you at about a three, okay?

                Mr. Hankey looks confused.
            He hops up onto the film chairman's podium.

                        MR. HANKEY
        Uh, folks, please, little towns like this simply aren't
            meant for big events. We love havin' visitors, but
        golly, too many of ya is hurtin' our ecosystem. Besides,

folks, film festivals shouldn't be about what celebrities are coming, or what film is gonna get sold. It should be about people getting together and watching movies, and about people who can never get their movies seen having a chance to have it watched, if only once. A good film festival should be something where you all say 'Aw, let's forget about lawyers and agents and studios and celebrities. Let's forget all those things for just a while, and just watch some new art.'

The Hollywood people look at each other.

Kyle smiles. Mr. Hankey smiles back.

                    FILM CHAIRMAN
            I HAVE HAD ENOUGH OF YOU!!!

The Film Chairman grabs Mr. Hankey, and throws him across the room -

                         KYLE
                         NO!

Mr. Hankey smacks hard against the opposite wall, leaving a small stain, and then falls lifeless to the floor.

                    FILM CHAIRMAN
            Now as I was saying, this shall usher
            in a whole new decade of...

As the chairman continues, the boys look at Mr. Hankey's limp body.

                         KYLE
                       (Crying)
            Oh, he's dead! Mr. Hankey's dead!!

                         CHEF
            Well, this worked once before...

Chef takes out a pile of his salty balls. He drops a LOT of them into Mr. Hankey's mouth.

Mr. Hankey is still for a few seconds, but then starts to move.

Suddenly, Mr. Hankey picks himself up and looks angrily at the chairman, who continues his speech.

                    MR. HANKEY
Thanks, Chef! Your big chocolate balls are just the trick!

Mr. Hankey takes off his sailor's cap, and replaces it with the Sorcerer's Apprentice hat from Fantasia. As the music from that scene begins, (what was it?) Mr. Hankey starts to bob up and down rhythmically.

                    STAN
        What the hell is he doing?

                    KYLE
            I don't know.

Just like Mickey Mouse did in the film, Mr. Hankey raises
    his hands to the music like a magician. When he does,
            thunder and lightning strike and -

        - from a sewer grill on the street,
        shit comes flying out in a large wave.

                    CARTMAN
                    Wow!!

        A group of about ten Hollywood types get
            doused in the magical shit.

                HOLLYWOOD TYPE
                OH MY GOD!!!

    Again Mr. Hankey throws up his hands, and again
            there is thunder and lightning.

        This time, a great wave of poo emerges from
                a nearby porta-potty.

    It heads right for another group of Hollywood types.

            HOLLYWOOD TYPE (cont'd)
                It smells, it smells!!!

But they cannot run fast enough, the poo catches up with
            them and douses them completely.

    Now everyone in the area panics and starts to run.

        The film chairman dashes for his Mercedes.

                INT. MERCEDES

    He and Phyllis jump in. The film chairman turns
            the key - but it won't start.

                    PHILLIS
        Come on!! The Poo is COMING!!!

                FILM CHAIRMAN
                I'm trying dammit!!

            ANGLE - MR. HANKEY

He throws his arms in another direction, and a great and
    mighty shit storm takes out the Planet Hollywood sign.

        The huge sign collapses right on top of the
            film chairman in his Mercedes.

CHEF'S SALTY CHOCOLATE BALLS

Everything is doused in shit as the chairman and
Phillis drown to their deaths.

HOLLYWOOD TYPE
Let's get the out of this town!

All the film people run away as fast as they can.

EXT. SOUTH PARK - NIGHT

The cars all pull out as fast as possible, suddenly
leaving South Park as peaceful and quiet as it once was.

EXT. POO-COVERED PLANET HOLLYWOOD - NIGHT

The music stops and Mr. Hankey relaxes and looks around
at the massive amounts of shit that cover everything.

MR. HANKEY
Gosh, I guess I don't know my own strength!

KYLE
You did it, Mr. Hankey! You got rid of all the film people!!

TOWNSPEOPLE
Hooray!!

MAYOR
(Sarcastic)
Oh yeah, now all we have is a town
covered in shit. This is MUCH better.

MR. HANKEY
I couldn't have done it without you Kyle! Kisses.

Mr. Hankey jumps into Kyle's arms and gives him a big kiss.

WENDY
Stan, I'm sorry I dragged you to all
those independent films.

STAN
Oh, that's okay, Wendy. I forgive you.

WENDY
Sometimes I forget that even though a few independent
films are great, most of them suck ass.

CARTMAN
Yes, and I've learned something too.

Everyone looks at Cartman.

CARTMAN
Being a sellout is sweet, because you make a lot
of money. And when you have money you don't have to
hang out with any poor ass losers like you guys.
Screw you guys, I'm going home.

COW DAYS

BY TREY PARKER & DAVID GOODMAN

INT. GAME SHOW - DAY

An elaborate, glitzy game show.
A couple, Tom and Mary, are standing on the stage.
A cheesy Game Show Guy holds an index card.

GAME SHOW GUY
Well Tom and Mary, you've made it to the final round.
Are you ready to play for the grand prize?

TOM AND MARY
We're ready, Bob!

GAME SHOW GUY
Any particular prize you're hoping for?

MARY
Well, Hawaii's nice, but Tahiti would be fun too!

TOM
Aw, anywhere'd be great!

GAME SHOW GUY
Polynesian diggidies, I wish you luck.
(Reading from the card)
Here we go... What is the thin flap of skin that runs
from the base of the penis to the scrotum?

A clock starts ticking. Tom and Mary think.

TOM
Oh, oh, wait wait, I KNOW this!

Finally Mary shouts it out -

MARY
The upper vascular hood?

The clock stops... silence...

GAME SHOW GUY
I'm sorry... BUT YOU'RE ABSOLUTELY RIGHT!!!

Game show MUSIC and applause.
Tom and Mary scream and hug.

GAME SHOW GUY
Fred, tell 'em what they've won!!

ANNOUNCER
Tom and Mary, put on your cowboy hats because you're
going to beautiful SOUTH PARK COLORADO!!!

Tom and Mary suddenly stop jumping
and look at each other, confused.

MARY
Where?

ANNOUNCER
That's right! Just in time for 'Cow Days,' the world's
forty-fifth biggest rodeo and carnival!!

Slides of South Park are shown with rodeo
events and lots of people celebrating.

ANNOUNCER
Every fall, South Park celebrates Cow Days and YOU'RE
going to be a part of it! You'll stay at the fabulous Super
7 hotel on Bernard Road, and enjoy festivities including
prizes, rides and of course the world famous 'Running of
the Cows!' Congratulations Tom and Mary!!

GAME SHOW GUY
Well Tom, Mary you must be very excited!

Tom and Mary just stand there for a minute.
Finally, Tom speaks.

TOM
What was second prize again?

GAME SHOW GUY
That's all for now! See you tomorrow on
'Ooh! What the Hell is That?!'

The audience all yells 'Ooh, What the
Hell is That?' with him.

MARY
Aw, shit.

EXT. SOUTH PARK - DAY

The whole town is gathered for a gala event.
Large banners read '14th Annual Cow Days!!'

EXT. RODEO STADIUM - DAY

A huge crowd is gathered to watch the rodeo.

MAYOR
Ladies and gentlemen, I am pleased to kick off the 14th
ANNUAL South Park Cow Days!!!

The townspeople all cheer.
Tom and Mary are in the crowd, dressed
in Cow Days regalia - horn hats and
Cow Days T-shirts.

MAYOR
As most of you know, Cow Days is when we all get together
to celebrate and thank the noble, gentle cow.

The townspeople cheer some more.

MAYOR
And now the chairman of Cow Days, Jimbo Kern!!

Jimbo takes the stage.

JIMBO
This year's a very special Cow Days,
because we are revealing our all new
COW MEMORIAL which will live forever
in South Park from this day forward.
Release the curtain!!

There is a gigantic, 60-foot-tall mass covered
in red curtain. Suddenly, the curtain drops,
revealing a giant, golden Cow Statue.

The crowd goes wild.

Just then, a large clock on the cow's chest strikes One,
and the cow's giant mouth opens -

COW STATUE
Moo.

The crowd goes even wilder.

MARY
This is the most ridiculous thing I've ever seen.

TOM
Now Mary, this is our only vacation for years.
We have to make the best of it.

MARY
Oh, you're right. I'm sorry, honey.
We just need to stay positive!!

The Mayor gets back on the microphone.

MAYOR
Now get out to the carnival and enjoy
the AMAZING RIDES and the WONDERFUL GAMES!!

INT. CARNIVAL - DAY

BOOTH GUY
Hey come on over here kids, win fabulous prizes!

The boys walk up to the booth.

KYLE
Wow, dude! Check it out! We can win
Terrance and Phillip dolls!!

Hanging from the booth are tons of crappy
Terrance and Phillip dolls.

STAN
Are those the real Terrance and Phillip dolls?
They look all crappy.

KYLE
Yeah, they look like cheap rip-offs.

BOOTH GUY
Sure they're real. They're even made in Canada.

STAN
Really?

BOOTH GUY
Yeah, look, they're even signed by
Terrance and Phillip themselves-

He flips the tag over and the sloppily handwritten
tag reads 'Terense and Phillup.'

CARTMAN
WOW!!

KYLE
Dude, that kicks ass!!

CARTMAN
Oh, dude! I gotta win those! How much to play?

BOOTH GUY
Five dollars for three balls.

CARTMAN
Five dollars?! Jesus Christ!

BOOTH GUY
Don't worry, kid, it's easy. You just gotta put one ball
through Jennifer Love Hewitt's mouth.

There is a big real-life photo of Jennifer Love Hewitt
with a huge hole cut out where her mouth should be.

CARTMAN
That's easy!

Cartman throws down five bucks.

BOOTH GUY (cont'd)
Okay, we got a playa!

The guy hands Cartman the balls.

CARTMAN
Alright, check it out!

Cartman throws the first ball.
It smacks Jennifer in the eye.

CARTMAN
Dammit!

BOOTH GUY
It's okay, son, you still have two balls to try
and get through her yapper.

Cartman winds up with the other ball.
He's determined and pissed.

CARTMAN
TAKE THIS JENNIFER LOVE HEWITT!!

Cartman throws the ball and hits
Jennifer in the other eye.

KYLE
You suck, Cartman!

CARTMAN
I'd like to see you do better!!

KYLE
Give me that!

Kyle takes the last ball, winds up and throws it.

KYLE
HEY! It hit her right in the mouth!

BOOTH GUY
It's gotta go THROUGH her mouth.

KYLE
But it-

BOOTH GUY
Sorry, kid. Try again! Just five more dollars!

KYLE
Here, give me some money Cartman!

Cartman thinks and then just busts out laughing.

KYLE
Lend me money fat boy!

CARTMAN
I only have three dollars left asshole.

KYLE
Damn it, come on. I'll try to get more money from my mom.

EXT. COW DAYS FAIRGROUNDS - DAY

A horde of townspeople are gathered in the streets of
South Park. Jimbo is on a small stage.

JIMBO
Okay everybody, it's time for the running of the cows!!

But the townspeople are cheering wildly.

Kyle and the boys run up to Mr. & Mrs. Broflovski.

KYLE
Mom, give me some money.

KYLE'S MOTHER
Kyle what are you doing here? This is very dangerous.

KYLE
I need $17 so we can win Terrance & Phillip dolls.

KYLE'S MOTHER
Kyle get back into the carnival this instant,
you can't be out on the streets!

KYLE
I will if you give me money.

KYLE'S MOTHER
Okay, here.

CARTMAN
Sweet!

JIMBO
Okay everybody, okay, settle down.

JIMBO
Now I know you're all anxious to get
to the running of the cows -

Now the townspeople go crazy.

JIMBO
But let me remind you, those brave souls who have decided
to run against the cows through town do so at their
own risk. I don't think I have to remind you that
three people died at last year's running of the cows.
With that said - LET'S ROCK AND ROLL!!!

The townspeople go crazy and all stand by, ready to run.

JIMBO
Everybody ready to run?!

JIMBO
RELEASE THE COWS!!!

Everyone starts SCREAMING and running as fast as they
can. The large cattle gate opens, and in a flurry -
Nothing happens. The cows just wander out slowly
and start eating grass. Most of the cows just
stand where they were.

Scene 065 | Panel | BG

Location/Time

Dialogue

Action/Efx

Trans.

27

Scene 066 | Panel | BG

Location/Time

Dialogue (10)

An- People run in every direction.

Action/Efx

But meanwhile, people are running as fast as they can.

Trans.

24

Scene 067 | Panel | BG S14046

Location/Time

Dialogue

JIMBO
THEY'RE LOOSE!! RUN NED!!!

Action/Efx

Trans.

31

Scene 068 | Panel | BG

Location/Time

Dialogue

Action/Efx

Trans.

→

Scene 068 CONT. | Panel | BG

Location/Time

Dialogue

Action/Efx

Ned runs into a telephone pole

Trans.

30

Scene 069 | Panel | BG

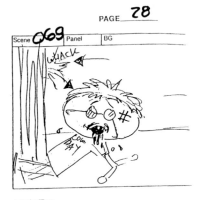

Location/Time

Dialogue

Action/Efx

and smashes his face in.

Trans.

23

But meanwhile, people are running as fast as they can.

JIMBO
THEY'RE LOOSE!!

Ned runs into a telephone pole and smashes his face in.

Another townsperson looks behind him as he runs, and doesn't see a large spike that he impales himself on.

It's a mess. People running and screaming and killing themselves and the cows aren't even chasing them.

JIMBO
Yee-ha!

Everyone runs and screams some more. One guy runs up to a cow with a bright red shirt. The cow looks at the guy and the guy runs screaming.

INT. CARNIVAL - DAY

A wide establishing of the fairgrounds.

The boys are walking through the rides.

KYLE
Okay, we've got fifteen dollars between us.
That means we get nine balls to throw.

CARTMAN
I only need one, dude. I only need one...

The boys walk past a shitty looking haunted house.

RECORDED VOICE
Come one, come all! Get in line now
for the CHAMBER OF FARTS.

STAN
What's that?

RECORDED VOICE
Dare you enter the Chamber of Farts?

CARTMAN
How much is it?

ATTENDANT
Just three tickets, boys.

RECORDED VOICE
Dare you enter the Chamber of Farts?

KYLE
Is it like a haunted house or something?

                    MICROPHONE GUY
                Sure, it's very scary.

                      CARTMAN
        Let's see... Each ticket is a dollar so three
            tickets is like... two twenty-five.

                        KYLE
            No, we can't, dude. We have to win the
                Terrance and Phillip dolls!

                      CARTMAN
            Aw come on you guys, we still have
                plenty of money left over.

                        KYLE
                You better be right, dude.

                      CARTMAN
                      I'm right.

            The boys head to the ticket line.

EXT. CHAMBER OF FARTS - DAY

        The boys are all sitting in a little, crappy moving car.
            An attendant lowers a bar across their laps.

                     ATTENDANT
            Keep your hands inside at all times.

                        KYLE
                        Okay!

                The car starts to move,
            it goes through a set of double doors.

INT. CHAMBER OF FARTS

            Crappy quality, spooky music plays.

                       VOICE
        So... The Chamber of Farts has another victim, eh?

        It's very dark now. The boys look around a bit scared.

                       VOICE
        Don't be afraid they're aren't any ghouls here...
                    Only FARTS!!!

        Suddenly, the boys' car turns and comes to a stop as a
        light shines on a pair of really bad wax dummies.

            There is a recorded SCREAM and then one
                of the wax dummies farts.

                      CARTMAN
                  Aw, Goddamnit!

The car moves on.

STAN
What the hell was that?

RECORDED VOICE
Perhaps you need some MORE FARTS!!

The car again spins around, this time facing
a wax dummy of a woman.

Again, a short, quiet fart sounds and
the little car moves on.

EXT. CHAMBER OF FARTS

The car exits through a set of double doors.

ATTENDANT
Alright, boys, ride's over.

KYLE
That was the dumbest ride I've ever seen!!

STAN
Yeah, what the hell kind of carnival company are you?!

CARTMAN
I don't know what you guys are talking about,
that scared the crap out of me.

KYLE
That was a waste of money Cartman.

CARNIVAL GUY
Hey if you guys want a great ride, get
in this line, it's only seven tickets.

KYLE
We can't. We're saving our money for the balls in
Jennifer Love Hewitt's mouth game.

CARTMAN
Kyle will you relax, you pinkeye! We have plenty of
money. Come on you guys it'll be sweet.

EXT. COW DAYS FAIRGROUNDS - DAY

The golden cow statue is standing majestically.

One of the cows slowly makes his way over
to the large golden cow statue.

The cow stares at it.
The statue seems to stare back.

Finally, clock on the golden cow strikes two o'clock
and it lets out a deep, meaningful moo.

                          COW STATUE
                          Mooo.

              The cow looks at the statue in
              amazement and lets out a moo.

                            COW
                          Mooo.

          Two other cows slowly join him, staring at
                the large wooden cow in awe.

                    INT. CARNIVAL - DAY

            The boys are standing in a long line.

                           KYLE
                This ride better be good.

                           STAN
              Yeah, this line is WAY too long!

                          CARTMAN
              I think we're almost to the end.

                           KYLE
          We better be. We've been in line for almost an hour.

            Finally, the boys reach the end of the line,
                        and walk out.

                           STAN
                       Here we go.

                           KYLE
                        Finally!

                       CARNIVAL GUY
                Did you enjoy the ride?

                The boys look confused.

                           STAN
                       What ride?

                           KYLE
                         Yeah.

                       CARNIVAL GUY
                  This was the line ride.
          A real-life simulator of a long line.

          PULL BACK to reveal a big sign that reads 'Line Ride.'

                           KYLE
              Oh, you've gotta be kidding me!

CARNIVAL GUY
That's five tickets, thank you very much.
Come see us again soon!

STAN
My ass we will!!

The boys walk off, pissed.

KYLE
Well Cartman, this is just my opinion, but I think the
line ride sucked donkey balls.

STAN
Yeah, let's not ride that ride again.

CARNIVAL GAL
Would you like to buy a photo of you
boys enjoying the line ride?

She opens up a photo that reads 'Line Ride MEMORIES!'
and inside is a picture of the boys
standing in line, looking bored.

CARTMAN
How much?

CARNIVAL GAL
Just three dollars.

CARTMAN
Oh that's pretty sweet.

Cartman pays her. She gives him the picture.

KYLE
You dumbass Cartman!

CARTMAN
What?! This is cool!

KYLE
No it's not cool!

CARTMAN
It's COOL!

The boys are again in front of the throw the balls in
Jennifer Love Hewitt's mouth game.

BOOTH GUY
Can I help you boys?

KYLE
We're gonna try to win those Terrance
and Phillip dolls again.

BOOTH GUY
Okay five dollars for three balls.

KYLE
How much do we have left Cartman?

No answer from Cartman.

KYLE
HOW MUCH DO WE HAVE LEFT CARTMAN?

CARTMAN
Uh, three dollars.

KYLE
What! You said we had plenty of money Cartman.

CARTMAN
Yeah, but I didn't take into account
the fact that I suck at math.

Kyle charges Cartman, knocks him over and
starts beating the shit out of him.

KYLE
You son of a bitch...

CARTMAN
Aaaahhh.

COMMERCIAL BREAK

EXT. COWDAYS FAIRGROUNDS - DAY

KYLE
Well, Cartman, thanks to you we don't have any money
left to win the Terrance and Phillip dolls!

CARTMAN
Well, I'm sorry.

STAN
Sorry's not good enough, what are you gonna do about it?

CARTMAN
Hey, I bet Kenny has some food stamps on him.

KENNY
Mrmph morm mmrmp.

STAN
Sir, will you take food stamps for three balls.

The guy thinks.

BOOTH GUY
Sure, as long as they're good.

KYLE
Give 'em your food stamps Kenny!

KENNY
Nuh-uh.

KYLE
Come on, dude, I can do it, I'm SURE!

KENNY
Mph rmph rm rmph rm!

CARTMAN
Dammit Kenny don't be such a food stamp hog!
Share with the rest of your friends!

Kenny sighs and hands them over. The booth guy
takes them and hands Kyle three balls.

KYLE
Okay, here we go...

Kyle winds up... And throws a ball right into
Jennifer's mouth. But it bounces off.

KYLE
HEY! That was right on target!

BOOTH GUY
Sorry, kid. Try again.

Kyle throws the second ball,
again it bounces off her mouth.

KYLE
THAT DOES IT!! SHENANIGANS!!!!

Kyle turns around and screams into the crowd.

KYLE
SHENANIGANS!!!!

BOOTH GUY
What are you doing?

KYLE
I'm declaring shenanigans on you!
This game is rigged!

BOOTH GUY
Shenanigans?

Officer Barbrady walks up.

OFFICER BARBRADY
What's all the hoo-ha?

                        KYLE
        Officer Barbrady, I want to declare
        shenanigans on this carnival operator.

                  OFFICER BARBRADY
                        Why?

                        KYLE
        This game is fixed! The balls are bigger than
        Jennifer Love Hewitt's mouth!

                  OFFICER BARBRADY
        If that is true, then your declaration of shenanigans is
        just. What do you have to say, carnival operator?

                     BOOTH GUY
             Look, the kid was really close.
        He still has another ball left. Let's try again son...

        As he says this, the booth guy trades the ball under
        the counter for another, obviously smaller one.

                     BOOTH GUY
                   Here you go.

             Kyle takes the ball and tosses it.
        It easily goes through Jennifer's mouth.

                     BOOTH GUY
        There! You see! We have a WINNA!!!

                        KYLE
                   It worked!

                  OFFICER BARBRADY
        Young man, you can't just go declaring shenanigans on
        innocent people. That's how wars get started.

                        STAN
             Sorry officer butt-baby.

                  OFFICER BARBRADY
                   Barbrady.

                        STAN
        Oh, I'm sorry, what did I say?

                  OFFICER BARBRADY
             You said butt-baby.

        The boys all laugh.

        Barbrady walks away.

                     BOOTH GUY
        Okay, kid. You won. You get to pick between the Barbie
        pocket mirror and the Bon Jovi toothpick.

KYLE
No, dude, I want the Terrance and Phillip dolls up there.

BOOTH GUY
Oh, no no no, you gotta win seven times to earn those.

KYLE
WHAT?!?!

BOOTH GUY
You win seven Bon Jovi toothpicks, then you can trade
'em in for the Terrance and Phillip dolls.

KYLE
You dirty son of a bitch, you never
told us that we had to...

BOOTH GUY
Step on up!! Just five dollars to play!!

The boys walk away, dejected.

KYLE
Dammit, I have to have those dolls.

STAN
This is hopeless. We're never gonna
have enough money to win.

Kyle stops at a large poster that reads 'Cow Days Bull
Riding Contest!!' and '$5,000 Grand Prize!!'

KYLE
Wait a minute! I've got it! The bull
riding contest! Cartman could ride a bull
and try to win five thousand dollars!

KYLE
Think about it, dude. Five thousand dollars... That's...
one thousand set of balls, that's three THOUSAND balls!
We'd have to win enough to get the dolls!

CARTMAN
What the hell makes you think Cartman rides a bull?

KYLE
Because you spent all of our money on those stupid rides
fatass! Now either you're getting on a bull or I'm
gonna break your fuckin' head open.

CARTMAN
Okay, I'll get on the bull.

KYLE
Alright now come on, you have to practice.

STAN
He really wants those dolls.

CARTMAN
I guess, damn.

EXT. CHAMBER OF FARTS - DAY

Tom and Mary come out of the ride.

MARY
That ride wasn't very good.

TOM
Now Mary, you promised me we'd try to have a good time.

MARY
You're right. I'm sorry honey.
I'll try and have a good time.

EXT. COW DAYS FAIRGROUNDS - DAY

The golden cow statue is standing majestically.

After a few seconds, we reveal that about
fifteen cows are gathered at the foot of
the statue, looking up in awe.

The cows just sit there and stare for a long time.
The statue does nothing. Until finally, the clock strikes
two, and the giant mouth of the cow drops open.

STATUE
Moo... Moo...

The cows all get wide eyes.
They lift their heads in unison.

COWS
Moo... Moo!

The cows wait for another response... but get none.

Three other cows walk into frame.
They stop when they see the statue.

EXT. BAR - NIGHT

Establishing.

INT. BAR - NIGHT

The boys are gathered around a mechanical bull.
Cartman is sitting on top of it.

STAN
Alright, this mechanical bull is gonna help you
practice for the real thing, Cartman.

CARTMAN
Hey, this is sweet.

KYLE
You gotta try and stay on for TEN SECONDS, okay Cartman?

CARTMAN
I'll try, ten seconds is a long time.

STAN
We'll start on the slowest setting and
work our way up. Ready? Go!

Kenny hits the switch.

Cartman is IMMEDIATELY flung off the bull,
across the bar, and into a pinball machine.

CARTMAN
AGH! SON OF A BITCH!!

STAN
(To Kyle)
How long was that?

Kyle is looking at a stopwatch.

KYLE
That wasn't quite ten seconds.

STAN
DAMMIT!!

The boys walk over to the pinball machine,
where Cartman is lying in horrible pain.

STAN
That wasn't ten seconds, Cartman!
You have to do better than that!

CARTMAN
(Lying on his back)
You guys... Seriously... My back...

KYLE
Get back on, fat ass! You have to
practice...

CARTMAN
Seriously... Help... Screw you guys... Hate you guys...

KYLE
What'd you say, Cartman?

CARTMAN
H...Hate you guys...

KYLE
I think he said he wants to practice
on a real bull.

> CARTMAN
> H...Hate you guys...

EXT. SOUTH PARK - DAY

An empty field with mountains in the background.

Nothing is visible in the frame, but we hear a sound.

> Screek...

> Screek...

> Screek...

Finally, the large golden cow statue is slowly pushed
in from the left side of frame. It scoots it slowly,
scraping the ground as it goes.

After it is pushed in far enough,
we see that the cows, a few dozen of them,
are pushing the statue with their noses.

Their progress is very slow.

EXT. CORRAL - DAY

The boys are gathered around a very old bull, which is in
its tiny wooden pen. Cartman is sitting on it.

> RANCHER
> Be careful with old Bob, here. He ain't much for
> riding anymore, but he's all I got.

> KYLE
> Well, he'll have to do. Cartman has to
> get in some practice with a real bull.

> RANCHER
> Well, have fun boys.

The rancher walks off.

> KYLE
> Okay, Cartman, you ready?

> CARTMAN
> No.

> KYLE
> OPEN THE GATE!!

Kenny pulls a rope and the wooden door swings open.

Old Bob very slowly walks out. Cartman relaxes, seeing
that this ride is going to be very easy.

CARTMAN
Alright, get down. This is my kind of bull ride.

Old Bob heads over to the other side
of the corral, away from the boys.

KYLE
That bull sucks, he's not even bucking or anything!

Cartman is still enjoying his ride.

CARTMAN
Yeah, this is sweet...

Kyle leans down and picks up some snow.
He packs it into a ball.

STAN
What are you gonna do?

KYLE
(Aiming)
Hit the bull in the balls with a snowball.

STAN
Oh... Yeah, that's a good idea.

Kyle throws the snowball and it hits the
bull square in the nuts.

Immediately the bulls eye's pop out and it
start bucking and snorting like a real bull.
Cartman holds on for dear life.

CARTMAN
AGAGH!!!

KYLE
That's better.

STAN
Hold on, Cartman!

Cartman is being tossed and thrown every which way.

CARTMAN
AGAHGAAHGH!!! SERIOUSLY YOU GUYS!! DO SOMETHING!!!!!
STOP THIS CRAZY THING!!!

Cartman finally crashes to the ground,
face down, right in front of Kyle and Stan.

KYLE
Get up, Cartman, you're still not staying on long enough.

No answer... Cartman just lies there face down.

>   STAN
>   Come on, Cartman!

No reply.

>   KENNY
>   Mph hm Mmm! Mrm rm Mphmph!

>   KYLE
>   No we didn't kill him, he's still breathing.

Kyle kicks Cartman.

>   KYLE
>   Get up!... Get up!

Finally, Cartman picks himself up off the dirt.
He looks really bad.

>   STAN
>   You okay, dude?

>   KYLE
>   Cartman... Hello... Hello...

>   STAN
>   Dude, I think we broke him.

The boys look at each other.

EXT. HOSPITAL - DAY

The boys are in the waiting room. The doctor comes out.

>   DOCTOR
>   Boys, I'm afraid your fat little
>   friend has suffered head trauma.

>   STAN
>   What's the matter with him?

>   DOCTOR
>   Well, apparently he thinks he's a
>   Vietnamese prostitute named Ming Lee.

>   KYLE
>   Oh...

>   STAN
>   But can he still ride a bull?

>   DOCTOR
>   What?

>   KYLE
>   We need him to win the bullriding contest
>   so we can get Terrance and Phillip dolls,
>   can he still do it?

DOCTOR
No, boys, you need to take him home
and let him get plenty of sleep.

KYLE
DAMMIT!

The boys walk over to Cartman in the hospital bed.

STAN
Cartman, Cartman, can you hear me?

CARTMAN
Pu lou, sher shay?

KYLE
WHAT?!!!!

CARTMAN
Pu lou, sher shay shy lee.

STAN
Oh he's fine dude!

KYLE
You think?

CARTMAN
Pu lou, sher shay shy lee.

STAN
Oh yeah dude, let's get his ass to the rodeo.

EXT. ANOTHER PART OF THE FAIRGROUNDS.

Jimbo stands at the stage with a microphone.

JIMBO
Alright, dammit!! We are not going to stand for this!!
Now whoever stole our golden cow memorial -
we're gonna find you and KILL YOU!!!

The townspeople all look at each other... Silence...

JIMBO
(Suddenly nice)
Alright, how about this; whoever took the sacred cow, just
please return him, and there'll be no questions asked...

The Townspeople remain silent.

Still silence. Tom and Mary look at each other.

JIMBO
Wait a minute... You folks from out of town...
YOU'RE the only ones with a reason to take
our beloved cow memorial!!

MARY
Where are we going to put a six foot tall statue of a cow?

OFFICER BARBRADY
I think maybe you'll answer that downtown, tourists!!

Barbrady puts cuffs on Mary and Tom.

MARY
Oh my God!

EXT. COW DAYS FAIRGROUND - DAY

The boys are walking Cartman through the Carnival.

STAN
How's he doing?

KYLE
He still thinks he's a Vietnamese prostitute.

CARTMAN
Pu lou, sher shay?

STAN
Do you think he can he ride the bull?

Kyle looks at Cartman.

KYLE
Yeah, I think so.

STAN
Cool.

They walk a little further and pass a SOLDIER
guy in uniform with his wife. Cartman suddenly
freaks out and runs up to him.

CARTMAN
Hallo? Hallo, prease. Soldier boy -
Hallo. Soldier boy. Hray Soldier boy.

SOLDIER
Huh?

CARTMAN
Harro soldier boy. Me so horny! Me rove you long time!

SOLDIER
Go away, kid, you're grossing me out.

CARTMAN
(Angry)
Hallo, prease, prease hallo, hallo,
suckie suckie. Hallo, prease.

SOLDIER
Beat it kid. Come on honey.

A loud voice booms over the speakers.

ANNOUNCER
COME ONE COME ALL!! THE CHAMBER OF
FARTS HAS BEEN FIXED AND IS REOPENED!!

Just then a huge crowd of people rush by. The boys
struggle to get through the crowd.

STAN
Jesus, dude!

KYLE
Hey, where's Cartman?!

The boys look around, Cartman's gone.

STAN
Oh, hell!

KENNY
Mph rmph rmp rmhp!

STAN
Kenny, you go find Cartman! We have to
go sign him up for the bull ride.

KENNY
Mph mm.

INT. PRISON - DAY

Tom and Mary are in their little cell.

TOM
Oh, it's so cold here!

MARY
Where is that Sheriff? We need water!

TOM
Oh well, let's try to make the best of it, Mary.

MARY
You're right, we're not being positive...
At least we get some time alone...

TOM
Yeah, and at least we've got our health...

Just then, a rat scurries by in the background.

EXT. VALLEY - DAY

Two random cowboys are walking through a field.

RANDOM COWBOY #1
I tell you, Mitchell, I ain't never seen nothing like it.

RANDOM COWBOY #2
Where are they again?

RANDOM COWBOY #1
Just right up over this ridge...

The cowboys walk up to a ridge.
We TRACK with them from behind.
As we come to the edge we see a valley...
FILLED with cows. Hundreds of them.
And Bubba is at the head.
They are all just sitting and mooing.

RANDOM COWBOY #1 (cont'd)
That's what they been doing all morning. Just sitting
there and mooing. And more cows come all the time.

RANDOM COWBOY #2
Well I ain't never seen this before, neither. But I know
one thing, when cows start getting together it can't
be good. They might start formin' a cult.

RANDOM COWBOY #1
Hmmm, cow cult.

The cows all moo in unison.

COMMERCIAL BREAK

EXT. RODEO - DAY

A huge crowd has gathered at the stadium
(we could probably use a modified version of
the kids' football field) for the big rodeo.

There are clowns, horses and cowboys everywhere.

ANNOUNCER (V.O.)
Here it is! The granddaddy of 'em all!
The South Park Cow Days Rodeo!

The crowd goes wild.

ANNOUNCER (cont'd)
Let's begin the bull riding event, grand prize
five THOUSAND dollars.

ANGLE - CROWD

They're all cheering.

Stan and Kyle are waiting around. Kenny walks up, alone.

STAN
Kenny, where the hell is Cartman?!

KENNY
Mph mrm mm!

KYLE
He's up in like twenty minutes!!

KENNY
Mph rmph rm rmph rm!

CARTMAN
Herro, prease. Herro?

STAN
There he is!!

Stan points to a group of people. Cartman is in the
middle of them, now dressed like a Vietnamese prostitute.

CARTMAN
Suckie, suckie, five dara!!

EXT. SOUTH PARK POLICE DEPT. - DAY

Establishing.

INT. PRISON - DAY

Tom and Mary are still sitting in their cell.

EXT. RIDGE OVERLOOKING MEADOW - DAY

The two random cowboys lead Jimbo and Ned to the ridge
overlooking the multitudes of cows.

RANDOM COWBOY #1
Here they are, just like we told you.

EXT. DOWN IN MEADOW - DAY

The cows are all mooing together, when Jimbo
walks in front of the statue.

JIMBO
Okay, that's enough of that. You cows need to disperse!

The cows just meditate.

JIMBO
Alright... Bad cows! Do you hear me? BAD COWS!!

The cows make no move.

JIMBO
Alright, Ned. You're gonna have to bust out the whip!

Ned pulls out a large whip. He snaps it in the air.

NED
Hiya. Get along little doggies.

Ned cracks a whip on one of the cows.

The cows now all turn on Ned, eye him
menacingly and approach slowly.

The cows come closer.

NED
Bad cows... Stay... Stay.

The cows charge him.

NED
AGHAGAH!!!!

JIMBO
Holy Crow! Play dead, Ned!

EXT. RIDGE OVERLOOKING MEADOW - DAY

The two cowboys look at each other as Ned is
pummelled to death in the background.

RANDOM COWBOY #1
I reckon we should get some help.

RANDOM COWBOY #2
...I reckon.

EXT. RODEO - DAY

The crowd on hand is enormous.

ANGLE - RODEO BULL PENS

The boys are gathered around Cartman, who is dressed
like a Vietnamese prostitute, on his bull.

KYLE
Don't be nervous, Cartman, this is gonna be cake.

STAN
Yeah, and then those Terrance and
Phillip dolls will be OURS!

CARTMAN
Suckie suckie five dara!

ANNOUNCER
Up first, number 24, JACK McMACK!

The crowd cheers as Jack McMack, an average
cowboy gets ready to ride.

ANNOUNCER
THREE... TWO... ONE!

The gate opens and the bull bursts out with Jack on
board! The bull bucks and kicks. The crowd goes wild.

Finally, the bull bucks Jack high into the air.
Jack falls back down right onto the bull's horns.

The horns go right through Jack and out
through his chest. Jack immediately starts
spewing blood out of his mouth.

ANNOUNCER
Oh, that's gonna cost him a point deduction!

The boys are staring on, wide-eyed.
Cartman looks the most petrified of all.

ANNOUNCER
Up next, number fourteen, Ming Lee!!

Dramatic MUSIC STING. The boys look worried.

CARTMAN
Ten dara? Eight dara! You gimme EIGHT DARA, soldier boy!

ANNOUNCER
Here we go!!...

STAN
Dude, I'm having second thoughts about this.

KYLE
What'dya mean?

STAN
I'm starting to think that maybe it's wrong to put someone
who thinks they're a Vietnamese prostitute on a bull.

The boys think.

ANNOUNCER
Let 'er go!!

Suddenly, the gate swings open and the bull
storms out, bucking up and down violently.

CARTMAN
AGH! PER LANG SHER SHAY! SUCKIE SUCKIE!!

KYLE
HANG ON, CARTMAN!!

The bull desperately tries to buck Cartman off,
but he's holding fast.

213

Scene **366** | Panel | BG

Location/Time

Dialogue

Action/Efx
Suddenly, the gate swings open
and the bull storms out,
bucking up and down violently.

Trans.

→

SOUTH PARK

366 cont

Scene | Panel | BG

Location/Time

Dialogue
CARTMAN
AGH! PER LANG SHER SHAY! SUCKIE SUCKIE!!

Action/Efx

Trans.

82

213   PAGE **153**

Scene **368** | Panel | BG

Location/Time

Dialogue
KYLE
HANG ON, CARTMAN!!

Action/Efx

Trans.

27

Scene **369** | Panel | BG

Location/Time

Dialogue

Action/Efx
The bull desperately tries to buck

Trans.

→

SOUTH PARK

369 cont

Scene **369** | Panel | BG

Location/Time

Dialogue

Action/Efx
Cartman off, but he's holding fast.

Trans.

→

213   PAGE **154**

Scene **369 cont** | Panel | BG

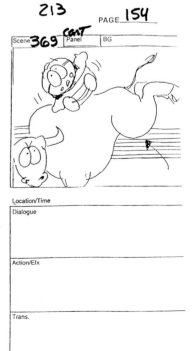

Location/Time

Dialogue

Action/Efx

Trans.

→

ANGLE - ANNOUNCER'S BOOTH

We see the announcer, holding a microphone, and another
guy sitting next to him.

ANNOUNCER
Wow, and this Vietnamese prostitute can really
ride a bull! I guess she's had a lot of practice,
if you know what I mean...

The friend looks bored.

ANGLE - CROWD

They're going wild for Ming Lee.

ANGLE - FIELD

Cartman is still riding the bull,
which hasn't slowed down at all.

CARTMAN
AGHGH!!! TEN DARA!! TEN DARA SOLDIER BOY!!

ANNOUNCER
She's setting a new world record!!

ANGLE - CROWD

Now they're all chanting.

CROWD
MING LEE! MING LEE! MING LEE!

ANGLE - FIELD

Cartman is finally thrown from the bull. He hits his
head on the ground when he falls.
Cartman picks himself up.

But just then, the bull rams into Cartman,
hitting him head first. The bull runs off.

Cartman picks himself up again.

STAN
Dude, that bull is gonna kill him!

KYLE
Go help him, Kenny!

Kenny starts toward the field, but then suddenly stops.

KENNY
(Angry)
Nuh-uh! Mph rmph rm rmph rm!!

Just then, the bull rams into the fence behind which Kenny is standing. The fence, the bull and Kenny all go flying off screen.

                    STAN
        Oh my God! They killed Kenny!

                    KYLE
             You bastards!!

ANGLE - ANNOUNCER'S BOOTH

                  ANNOUNCER
    And this brave little whore from the East has
    really put on a show for us today. The winner of
        the bull riding contest... MING LEE!!

            The crowd goes nuts.

        On the field, a helpful clown picks Cartman
        up and leads him to a large barrel.

                  CARTMAN
        Suckie, suckie? Only ten dara!

                    STAN
         We did it, dude! We did it!!

EXT. DOWN IN MEADOW - DAY

    The cows are standing around the statue. Just then from
    behind a ridge FBI agents pop up with machine guns.

                  FBI AGENT
         Freeze cows, the game is over!
      You will now return to your respective towns.

                   JIMBO
    You hear that cows? You're surrounded. There's no way out.

                  FBI AGENT
        You will now all march in an orderly
        fashion into this trailer. MOVE!

    The cows all just blankly stare at the agents. Just then
    one cow heads in the other direction towards a cliff.

                   JIMBO
        Hey where's she going? That's the
          wrong way you stupid cow.

    Like a lemming, the cow hurls itself off the cliff.

                  FBI AGENT
         Oh dear Jesus NO!!!

                   JIMBO
    NOOOO!!! They're killing themselves. Stop, PLEASE!!

One by one the cows jump off the cliff.

JIMBO
Can't we do anything? Oh God the
humanity Ned. The humanity...

FBI AGENT
This is the first mass cow suicide
I've seen in at least eight months.

INT. PRISON - DAY

Tom and Mary are still sitting in their cell.

INT. CARNIVAL - DAY

The boys walk up to the balls in Jennifer Love
Hewitt's mouth game, holding five thousand dollars.

BOOTH GUY
Oh, you boys are back again, huh?

STAN
Yeah. And we have FIVE THOUSAND DOLLARS THIS TIME!

KYLE
How many balls does that get us?

The booth guy's eyes grow wide.

CARTMAN
Ping lou der sher shay!

BOOTH GUY
I tell you what, boys... I'm gonna be really
nice and just TRADE you the five thousand
for the Terrance and Phillip dolls.

KYLE
You will?!

STAN
Wow! Why'd you get so cool all of a sudden?!

The Booth guy takes down the dolls and hands
them to the boys. Kyle hands over the money.

KYLE
We did it! You see, Cartman?
You won us the Terrance and Phillip dolls!

CARTMAN
Ten dara? Suckie, suckie?

The boys walk away, ecstatic.

KYLE
What should we do with them?

                    STAN
               We should -

But Stan's sentence is cut short when Phillip's head
     suddenly falls off and hits the ground.

                    KYLE
               What the...

Then Terrance's leg falls off.

                    STAN
     Dude! These dolls ARE cheap rip-offs!!!

                    KYLE
After all that?! SHANANIGANS!!! SHANANIGANS!!!!
               (Screaming)
          SHANANIGANS!!!!

A huge crowd of people gather around.

               OFFICER BARBRADY
               What's all this?

The carnival people (all the ride
operators and the Booth Guy) gather
at the other edge of frame.

                    KYLE
Officer Barbrady, I would like to reinstate my previous
shenanigans! This whole carnival is a rip-off!!

               MR. GARRISON
You know, excuse me, but I agree, these rides are really
stupid. Chamber of Farts isn't scary at all.

                    PRIEST
Yeah... And the food is TERRIBLE!!

               CARNIVAL GUY
Hey, it's just a stupid rodeo, what do you expect.

The townspeople and carnival people
all start yelling at each other.

               OFFICER BARBRADY
Okay, okay... Let's calm down... People of South Park,
do you declare shenanigans on the carnival people?

               TOWNSPEOPLE
               YES!!! YEAH!!

               OFFICER BARBRADY
Okay, carnival people, do you accept
this decree of shenanigans?

               CARNIVAL WOMAN
What the hell are you talking about?!

This whole town is screwy!

OFFICER BARBRADY
Well that settles it! EVERYBODY GRAB A BROOM!
IT'S SHANANIGANS!!!!!

The townspeople all grab brooms and start
beating the carnies senseless.

It is a massacre, as the unsuspecting carnival people had
no idea that shenanigans means all-out physical war.

EXT. FAIRGROUNDS - DAY

A bunch of townspeople are wheeling the huge wooden
cow clock back into its place at the fair.

MAYOR
You found it! You found the memorial!

JIMBO
Yup.

MAYOR
And the cows? Are they all back too?

JIMBO
They're dead Mayor, they're all dead.

MAYOR
What?

JIMBO
Oh it was awful. Cow after cow taking its own life.
And we could do nothing to stop them. Oh God.

MAYOR
Well perhaps one day cows will learn
that cults are never a good thing.

JIMBO
I hope so Mayor, I hope so.
God, I need a cold beer and a burger.

EXT. OUTSIDE THE FAIRGROUNDS - DAY

Jimbo and The Mayor are setting the wooden cow back
into place with the help of several others.

JIMBO
What's all the ruckus in there?

MAYOR
Sounds like somebody declared shenanigans.

JIMBO
Oh, hell, I'll have to run home and get my broom!

COMMERCIAL BREAK

EXT. SOUTH PARK POLICE DEPT. - DAY

INT. JAIL - DAY

Barbrady leads the carnival people into the jail.

OFFICER BARBRADY
Alright you damn carnival people,
into the jail with - Ooooh!!!

Barbrady does a double take when he sees that
Tom and Mary, now mostly skeletons with rats
on them, are still in prison.

JIMBO
Hey... Aren't those the people we at
first thought took the wooden cow?

OFFICER BARBRADY
Yeah...

MAYOR
Didn't we ever release them?!

JIMBO
I forgot all about 'em...

OFFICER BARBRADY
Me too.

MAYOR
Oh my God... Officer Barbrady,
you never had Tom and Mary in this cell!

OFFICER BARBRADY
I didn't?

MAYOR
No...no, in fact, they never came to South Park.
We've never heard of them.

Barbrady thinks.

OFFICER BARBRADY
Oh whew! I feel a lot better, then. Although I could
have SWORN that I HAD heard of them and they
starved to death in my prison...

EXT. FAIRGROUNDS - DAY

Kyle and Stan are playing with their
Terrance and Phillip dolls.

STAN
(As Phillip)
Say Terrance, let's look for treasure.

KYLE
(As Terrance)
Oh good idea Phillip, let's look for treasure.

Just then Cartman walks up to them.
He's back to his old self.

CARTMAN
What are you doing?

STAN
Oh, hey Cartman, how are you feeling?

CARTMAN
Oh, pretty good except I had the
weirdest dream last night.

STAN
Really? What about?

CARTMAN
Well, I dreamt that I was a poor Vietnamese girl,
and then you guys made me ride a big scary bull.
And then Leonardo DiCaprio gave me a spanking
for several hours. Hey, how did you guys win
all those Terrance and Phillip dolls?

KYLE
Oh, nowhere.

Kyle and Stan laugh.

CARTMAN
Wait a minute. You guys did make me ride that bull.

KYLE
No Cartman that was just a dream.

Just then a limo drives by and stops.

MAN IN LIMO
Bye Ming Lee. Thanks again.

The boys laugh.

CARTMAN
Oh, son of a bitch!!!!

GNOMES

BY MATT STONE, TREY PARKER & PAM BRADY

INT. CLASSROOM - DAY

MR. GARRISON
Settle down children...

The kids settle down.

MR. GARRISON
I have some difficult news... This is going to
make you all very sad... The school board is
considering firing me as your teacher.

The kids just sit there.

MR. GARRISON
There is a possibility that I will be let go,
and never allowed to teach you again.

Stan raises his hand.

MR. GARRISON
Yes, Stanly?

STAN
That's okay with us.

KYLE
Yeah.

KIDS
Yeah, we don't care.

MR. GARRISON
NO IT ISN'T IT MAKES YOU VERY SAD!!! Now, apparently the
school board thinks that I don't teach you anything
about current events, so tomorrow they're gonna have
you do presentations for the whole board...

The kids all moan.

MR. GARRISON
(Writing on chalkboard)
'Current Events in South Park.' Now I want
you all to read a newspaper or better yet
watch television, and come up with something
current in South Park to do a report on.

The kids moan louder.

MR. GARRISON
Now, this will be a group project, so I'm going to place
you all into groups of five. Let's see...

As Garrison calls out names, the camera MOVES
across the kids' faces to show who they are.

MR. GARRISON
Wendy, Bebe, Clyde, Pip and Token, you will be group one.

And group two will be... Stan, Kyle, Eric,
Kenny and... and... Tweek!

The Camera RUSHES OVER to Tweek, a very stressed out
little boy who shakes violently all the time and
looks like a strung-out heroin addict.

> TWEEK
> WAH!

> STAN
> Oh, not Tweek!

> KYLE
> We don't want to be in a group with Tweek!

Tweek shivers and shakes.

> MR. GARRISON
> There's nothing wrong with Tweek.
> I bet he'll do a great job in your group.

> TWEEK
> I can't take that kind of pressure!
> No, sweet Jesus, please!!!

> STAN
> Dude, we can't work with this kid.

> TWEEK
> AGH!

> MR. GARRISON
> That's what Chad Everett thought when the new female
> intern joined the cast of Medical Center. He thought,
> 'Who is this woman with her gazungas and high heels?
> What does she know of medicine?' Well, that intern
> soon saved Chad Everett's brother with a
> kidney transplant. So you see?

> KYLE
> No.

> MR. GARRISON
> Well, let me put it another way... You have to give your
> oral report to the entire South Park Town Committee
> tomorrow, and if it doesn't kick ass, and you make me
> look bad, Mr. Hat is gonna smack you bitches up.

The kids sit in shock.

> TWEEK
> WAH!

INT. TWEEK BROTHER'S COFFEE HUT

Mr. TWEEK stands behind the counter. He wears a name tag
so we know it is him. A customer walks in.

MR. TWEEK
Hello there customer!

MR. POSTUM
Hello, how are you today?

MR. TWEEK
Great! What can I get for you? Large coffee, small coffee?

MR. POSTUM
I'm actually interested in something else -

The man places a large briefcase on the counter.

MR. POSTUM
I'm John Postum from the Harbucks Coffee corporation.

MR. TWEEK
Oh... You're that corporate guy who's been calling.

MR. POSTUM
That's right. How come you don't call me back?
All we want to do is buy out your coffee shop here.

MR. TWEEK
Forget it. My store is not for sale.

MR. POSTUM
My company is prepared to make you a VERY generous offer -

Postum opens the briefcase. It's empty.

MR. POSTUM
This is a Cramsonite briefcase. All leather. It has four
compartments and a keyless lock. Interested?

MR. TWEEK
Oh, I don't think so. My coffee shop is worth a lot to me.

MR. POSTUM
Alright... how about 500,000 dollars?

MR. TWEEK
The answer is still no Mr. Postum. You see, when my father
opened this store thirty years ago, he cared only
about one thing, making a GREAT cup of coffee.

Mr. Tweek starts to walk.
Now he talks directly into the camera.

MR. TWEEK (cont'd)
Sure we may take a little longer to brew a
cup and we may not call it fancy names,
but I guess we just care a little more.

Now Mr. Tweek walks in front of a huge painting of a
green field. He picks up a handful of coffee beans.

MR. TWEEK (cont'd)
And that's why Tweek coffee is still homebrewed from the
finest beans we can muster. Yes, Tweek coffee is a
simpler coffee... For a simpler America.

A beat. Tweek's commercial appears to be over.
Postum picks up the briefcase.

MR. POSTUM
Well, that's too bad. We're just gonna have to open our
Harbucks right next door to you.

MR. TWEEK
But, that could put me out of business!

MR. POSTUM
Hey, this is a capitalist country, pal. Get used to it.

Mr. Postum walks out just as Barbrady walks in.

BARBRADY
Hello Mr. Tweek.

MR. TWEEK
Hi Officer Barbrady.

BARBRADY
Who was that?

MR. TWEEK
Oh, just some dong... What can I get for you?

BARBRADY
The usual.

Mr. Tweek slaps Officer Barbrady
in the face with a live cat.

Barbrady stands stunned for a second.

BARBRADY
Thanks, see you tomorrow.

MR. TWEEK
Bye, bye.

He leaves.

INT. CLASSROOM - DAY

The kids are all gathered in clusters.
The boys sit with Tweek in their group.

STAN
Okay... We have to do this stupid report so-

TWEEK
AGH!

STAN
- So let's figure out what to do it about.

The boys all think.

CARTMAN
How about we do it on that Raymond guy on T.V...
You know, everybody loves Raymond.

KYLE
No, Cartman we can't do it on Raymond AGAIN!
It has to be a current event in South Park.
Tweek, do you have any ideas?

TWEEK
WAH! Too much pressure!

STAN
Great. A lot of help you are, kid.

TWEEK
The gnomes!

KYLE
What?

TWEEK
We can do our report on the gnomes!

STAN
What gnomes?

TWEEK
The underpants gnomes! Those little guys that...
That come in your room late, late at night
and steal your underpants!

The boys think.

CARTMAN
Oh, so THAT'S where all my underpants go...

Stan and Kyle looks at Cartman.

KYLE
Dude, that's the dumbest thing I've ever heard.

STAN
Yeah, I've never seen any underpants gnomes!!

TWEEK
They come out at three thirty in the
morning... Most people aren't up then...
But I am. I can't sleep. Ever.

Tweek sniffles.

KYLE
Dude, we can't do a presentation on
underpants gnomes, Mr. Garrison will
fail us because you're making it up!!

TWEEK
No! Sleep at my house tonight! I'll prove it to you!

INT. TWEEK'S HOUSE - NIGHT

Tweek's parents are standing in the kitchen.

MR. TWEEK
They want me to sell the store. And it's so much money.

MRS. TWEEK
Some things are more important than money.
The people of South Park count on you to give
them that first cup of coffee every day.

MR. TWEEK
I know, but if they open a Harbucks right
next door, we might go out of business.
They really have my balls in a vice grip...

The boys and Tweek walk in.

TWEEK'S MOM
Oh, hello son! How was your day?

TWEEK
Aaaagaggh!

TWEEK'S MOM
That's good. Who are your little friends?

TWEEK
WHATDOYOUMEAN?!

KYLE
We're his oral report buddies.

STAN
Yeah, we have to stay up all night to write it.

TWEEK'S MOM
Well, have some coffee boys.
I'll brew up another pot for later.

She hands mugs of coffee out to the boys.

KYLE
Coffee? I don't think I like coffee.

TWEEK'S MOM
Oh, you'll like THIS coffee. It's fresh.

TWEEK'S DAD
Country Fresh. Like the morning after a rainstorm.

STAN
Kay... Maybe it'll help us figure out what to do our
report on. We have to present it to the entire
South Park Town Committee tomorrow.

Mr. Tweek gets an idea just as the boys all start
drinking from huge mugs of coffee.

MR. TWEEK
Oh, I've got one for you. How about doing a report
on how large corporations take over little,
family-owned businesses?

TWEEK'S MOM
Richard-

MR. TWEEK
No, I'm serious, hon. These boys should learn how The
Corporate Machine is ruining America. You see... I own a
coffee shop, and now a great, big multi-million dollar
company is going to move in and try to take all my
business. Which means I may have to shut down,
and sell my son Tweek into slavery.

TWEEK
AGH! SLAVERY!

MR. TWEEK
Yes, slavery.

STAN
Wow, that sucks, dude.

MR. TWEEK
They really have my balls in a salad shooter.

KYLE
We're already doing a paper on Tweek's underpants gnomes.

STAN
Yeah.

TWEEK'S MOM
Now Tweek, how many times do we have to tell you.
Your underpants are missing because you lose them,
not because of underpants gnomes.

TWEEK
AGHH!!

KYLE
Come on, you guys, we better get to work!

The boys all walk away.

217
ACT I pg9-11

SOUTH PARK

217   PAGE 45

Scene 100	Panel	BG

Location/Time   INT. TWEEKS HOUSE - TWEEK'S BEDROOM

Dialogue

KYLE
WOOHOO!!!

Action/Efx

Kyle jumps off the bed
into a pile of toys as Stan goes cruising by.
STAN
YES! THIS STUFF ROCKS!

Trans.

An— Jump behind the toys, Start Stan out of frame.

84

Scene 103	Panel	BG

Location/Time   INT. Bedrm

Dialogue

KYLE
TOTALLY DUDE! I FEEL AWESOME!!!

Action/Efx

Kyle pops his head out of the pile.

Trans.

42

Scene 104	Panel	BG

Location/Time   INT. Bedrm

Dialogue

KENNY
STAN
WHOOPEE!!!
Kenny runs from offscreen yell-
and runs SMACK into a the
NIGHTSTAND

(Knocking over LAMP.)

Trans.

An Animate to Stan's voice.

SOUTH PARK

PAGE

Scene 104 cont.	Panel	BG

Location/Time

Dialogue

Action/Efx

Special body.

Trans.

Scene 104 cont	Panel	BG

Location/Time

Dialogue

he gets up and continues to   run.

Action/Efx

(at camera)

An— Animate really bouncy.

Trans.

98

Scene 107	Panel	BG

Location/Time   INT. Bed REV.

Dialogue   (Kenny runs by.)

CARTMAN
YOU GUYS!! YOU GUYS!!! SERIOUSLY!!! CHECK
ME OUT!!! I'M A SORCERER!!!
BEKEW!! BEKEW!

Action/Efx

Cartman runs around in a circle
like a mad dog.

Trans.

122

MR. TWEEK
Okay, but corporate takeovers is a
much more fertile subject.

TWEEK'S MOM
Honestly, Richard, I don't see why you have to
preach to some eight year olds.

MR. TWEEK
Actually, honey, I think those little tykes are
just what we need... I've got an idea.

EXT. TWEEK'S HOUSE - NIGHT

It's late. We only hear birds chirping.

INT. TWEEKS HOUSE - TWEEK'S BEDROOM

The boys are in Tweek's with cups of coffee.

KYLE
(taking a drink)
Man, this stuff is strong.

STAN
It's kind of bitter.

Tweek is shaking in the corner.

TWEEK
What if my parents go out of business?! What'll I do?

KYLE
Don't worry about it.

TWEEK
But we'll starve and die like dogs!

CARTMAN
Tweek, Tweek, you can always go on welfare. Look at
Kenny's family... They're perfectly happy being poor
and on welfare, right Kenny?

KENNY
Mph mmph.

CARTMAN
Ha ha ha! You suck Kenny!

KYLE
Well, let's just try to finish all
this coffee so we can stay up.

INT. TWEEK'S BEDROOM - LATER

KYLE
WOOHOO!!!

SOUTH PARK 217 PAGE 49

Scene 110 CONT.	Panel	BG

Location/Time **Bed rm**

Dialogue

TWEEK
grounds....

Action/Efx

AN: PULL OUT COFFEE GROUNDS FROM BEHIND HIS BACK. STARING FORWARD

Trans.

29

Scene 111	Panel	BG S/A 109

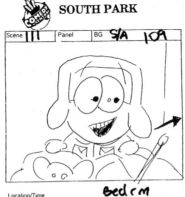

Location/Time **Bed rm**

Dialogue

KYLE
KILLER!

Action/Efx

AN: KYLE SHOULD START HOPING OUT OF THE TOYS IN THIS SHOT

Trans.

14

Scene 112	Panel	BG

Location/Time **Bed rm SIDE**

Dialogue

Action/Efx

Kyle runs over

Trans.

28

SOUTH PARK 217 PAGE 50

Scene 113	Panel	BG

Location/Time **Bdrm**

Dialogue

Action/Efx

and starts eating the grounds by the spoonful.

Trans.

AN: TWEEK STARING FORWARD

24

Scene 114	Panel	BG

Location/Time **Bdrm**

Dialogue

CARTMAN
Hey! Let me have some grounds!!

Action/Efx

AN: TWEEK STARING FORWARD

Trans.

30

Scene 115	Panel	BG

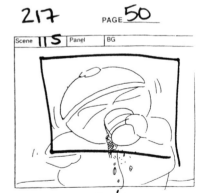

Location/Time **Bed rm**

Dialogue

TD - EATING Mouths

Action/Efx

Cartman pours the whole thing in his mouth

Trans

AN: HAVE SOME BEANS SPILLIN OUT OF HIS MOUTH TOO.

29

126

Kyle jumps off the bed into a pile of toys
as Stan goes cruising by.

STAN
YES! THIS STUFF ROCKS!

Kyle pops his head out of the pile.

KYLE
TOTALLY DUDE! I FEEL AWESOME!!!

STAN
WHOOPEE!!!

Stan runs SMACK into a wall.
He gets up and continues to run.

Cartman runs around in a circle like a mad dog.

CARTMAN
YOU GUYS!! YOU GUYS!!! SERIOUSLY!!! CHECK ME OUT!!!
I'M A SORCERER!!! BEKEW!! BEKEW!! CHECK ME OUT YOU GUYS!!

KYLE
Hey Tweek! Do you have any more of this stuff?!

Tweek is over in the corner, shivering and jittering.
He holds out a can of coffee grounds.

TWEEK
We just have grounds...

KYLE
KILLER!

Kyle runs over and starts eating
the grounds by the spoonful.

CARTMAN
Hey! Let me have some grounds!!!

Cartman pours the whole thing in his mouth and
promptly throws up all over the floor.

KYLE
GROSS CARTMAN! WHOOOPPPEEEE!!!!

Kyle runs off.

INT. TWEEK'S BEDROOM - LATER THAT NIGHT

The clock reads 3:26 a.m. and the kids are
all looking kind of shitty.

KYLE
Oof... My stomach hurts.

SOUTH PARK

217   PAGE 54

Scene 122 | Panel | BG

Location/Time Bedrm

Dialogue

Everyone freezes
No head & shaking

Action/Efx

Suddenly, some distant SINGING is heard.

Trans.

46

Scene 123 | Panel | BG

Location/Time Bd rm

Dialogue

STAN
What's that?!

KYLE
That's just Cartman's stomach dude.

Action/Efx

Trans.

49

Scene 124 | Panel | BG

Location/Time Bdrm

Dialogue

Action/Efx

Cartman is laying on his back.
He pukes straight up in the air

Trans.

→

SOUTH PARK

217   PAGE 55

Scene 124 CONT. | Panel | BG

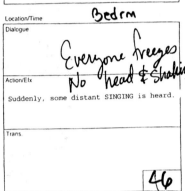

Location/Time Bdrm

Dialogue

CARTMAN (~~mumble~~)
I Don't feel so good.you.guys.

Action/Efx

and the puke lands all over his face.

Trans.

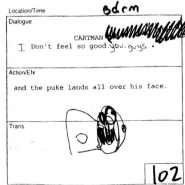

102

Scene | Panel | BG

Location/Time OH overhead

Dialogue

Action/Efx

Trans.

Scene 126 | Panel | BG

Location/Time Bd rm

Dialogue

Action/Efx

The singing suddenly grows louder
and louder Cartman turns
his head towards
Camera.

Trans.

45

STAN
Yeah, mine too. I wonder why.

A strange low-pitched noise is heard.

KYLE
Well, it's three thirty and I don't see any god
damned underpants gnomes, Tweek.

TWEEK
Agh! Maybe... Maybe it was all in my head!
Maybe I'm going INSANE! OH NO! I'm GOING INSANE!!

STAN
This is just great, we haven't gotten anything
done and we're totally SCREWED!

Just then, Tweek's father opens the door.

MR. TWEEK
How's the report going, boys?

STAN
Bad.

MR. TWEEK
Oh, do you need some more coffee?

The boys all moan.

Cartman is laying on his back. He pukes straight up in
the air and the puke lands all over his face.

CARTMAN
No more coffee...

Mr. Tweek walks in the room.

MR. TWEEK
Well, boys, I don't mean to pry but... If you want it,
I wrote your report for you.

The boys all light up (except for Cartman)

BOYS
YOU DID?!

MR. TWEEK
Yes, it's all about corporate takeovers.
Of course, you don't HAVE to use it...

STAN
NO! We'll use it!

MR. TWEEK
Alright, and it can be our little
secret about who wrote it, right?

                        KYLE
                        Sure!

While this happens we see Tweek hearing music,
looking around, and finally focusing on the
        closet with an open mouth.

                     MR. TWEEK
Now, when you give the report, just make sure
     that you read this part first, alright.

                       TWEEK
                  There they are!

No one pays attention to him, or to the fact that
a line of gnomes have entered the room and begun
     stealing underpants from Tweek's dresser.

                     MR. TWEEK
And then, someone should do the second part...
and really, really play it up. You know, really play
the sympathy angle, they'll like that. You'll probably,
     you know, get a passing grade for that.

Tweek points at the gnomes, looks at his dad,
           and then back to the gnomes.

                       TWEEK
   You guys, look, look you're missing it.

                 The gnomes leave.

                  TWEEK (cont'd)
             AGH! THEY TOOK 'EM AGAIN!!

                        KYLE
                   (To Mr. Tweek)
                   Thanks, dude!

                     MR. TWEEK
        My pleasure, good night boys.

                 Mr. Tweek leaves.

                        STAN
           Wow Tweek, your dad rocks.

                       TWEEK
       WHY DO THEY TORTURE ME LIKE THIS!!
       WHY CAN'T THEY LEAVE ME ALONE!!!

                        KYLE
  Damn it, what the hell is wrong with you Tweek!

                       TWEEK
        They took my underpants again...
     soon they'll want my blood... BLOOD!!!

ACT II

INT. SOUTH PARK COMMITTEE - DAY

This is just a large room. The South Park Committee sits
at a long table with microphones in front of them. (You
know, like the town meetings you see on public access.)

The boys are standing in front of the South Park
Committee, giving their presentation.

KYLE
And as the voluminous... corporate automaton
bulldozes its way through bantam America...

Cartman steps forward with his arms behind his back.

CARTMAN
What will become of the endeavoring American family?

Garrison rolls his eyes.

MR. GARRISON
I don't think they wrote this Mr. Hat!

STAN
Perhaps there is no stopping the corporate machine.

TWEEK
AGH!!

KYLE
And... that's our report... I guess.

MR. GARRISON
Well, boys, its obvious that you didn't even-

COMMITTEE CHAIR
GREAT JOB!!

The boys look shocked. So does Garrison.

MR. GARRISON
Yes, great job.

COMMITTEE CHAIR
Boys, you have really opened our eyes!
We didn't even know this was happening!

CARTMAN
Neither did we.

COMMITTEE CHAIR
Well, Mr. Garrison, it looks like we were
wrong about you. You really are teaching
these kids something.

MR. GARRISON
Yeah, well, I don't want to sound like
a dickhole, but I told you so.

COMMITTEE CHAIR
I am really moved... I say we follow these boys' cause!
Let's join them in the fight against corporate takeovers!!

The committee all stands up and cheers.

COMMITTEE CHAIR
Lead the way, boys!

KYLE
Huh?

TWEEK
AGH! Too much pressure!

EXT. HARBUCKS COFFEE HOUSE

The new Harbucks coffee place is BEING built
right next to the much smaller Tweek's coffee house.
A large banner reads 'OPENING SOON!'
Postum barks out commands to the building crew.

MR. POSTUM
Good! Good! Make sure that sign is
really bright and flashy, now!

Meanwhile, across the street, Mr. Tweek and
Mrs. Tweek are watching all of this.

MRS. TWEEK
My goodness, that's going to be
a huge coffee house, honey.

MR. TWEEK
Yes it is... They really have my balls in a juicemaker.

Just then, the boys walk up.

TWEEK'S DAD
Oh hello, son! Uh, how did your report go?

TWEEK
Wah!

KYLE
I think it went really good.
Those people really got into it.

MR. TWEEK
Really?! Well, son, you might have just saved the family
business! What do you have to say about that?!

TWEEK
I need coffee!

MR. TWEEK
I know how you boys feel. Sometimes a hot cup
of French Roast Amaretto is just what a man
needs to get him through the day -

Mr. Tweek walks off and puts his leg up on a stump.

MR. TWEEK
That smooth aroma and mild taste is what makes
Tweek's coffee so very special -

Percolating sounds start and light piano music.

MR. TWEEK (cont'd)
- Special like an Arizona sunrise or a juniper wet
with due... A light rain in the middle of a dusty
afternoon or a hug from your dear old auntie...

TWEEK
DAD!
The commercial ends abruptly.

MR. TWEEK
Huh?

TWEEK
The metaphors man.

MR. TWEEK
Oh sorry... Here you go.

Mr. Tweek hands his son some coffee.

KYLE
Hey, do ever think maybe you shouldn't
give your son coffee?

MRS. TWEEK
Like how do you mean?

KYLE
Like look at him. He's always shaking and nervous.

TWEEK
Aagh!

MRS. TWEEK
Oh that. He has ADD, Attention Deficit Disorder.
That's why he's so jittery all the time.

Just then, South Park committee comes rushing up.
Everyone is AD LIBBING angrily.

COMMITTEE CHAIR
Mr. Tweek! We've only just heard!

MR. TWEEK
Oh, hello Committee members, what a surprise...

Mr. Tweek smiles at his wife.

COMMITTEE CHAIR
So this is the corporate bulldozer
trying to push you off the map?

MR. TWEEK
Yes... How did you hear?

COMMITTEE MEMBER
These boys did an EXCELLENT report for us this morning.
They're so upset by this whole thing.

KYLE
My butt hurts.

COMMITTEE CHAIR
Don't worry, Mr. Tweek, this committee
is NOT going to let you be run out of
business by these bastards!

She turns to yell at Postum.

COMMITTEE CHAIR (cont'd)
You hear that?! You're not going to
get away with this you WHORE!!

In a super wide shot, Postum waves to her.

MR. POSTUM
Excuse me?

COMMITTEE MEMBER
Boys, we've talked it over, and we want
you to take your case to the MAYOR!

STAN
OUR case?

TWEEK
AGH! NO WAY, MAN! That is WAY too much pressure!!

MR. TWEEK
Oh, you'll do fine, son.

COMMITTEE MEMBER
Come on, boys, let's go!

The committee members leave,
dragging the boys with them.

CARTMAN
Aw, man! This sucks!

TWEEK
AGH!!

GNOMES

INT. MAYOR'S OFFICE - DAY

The boys are standing with the committee
in front of the Mayor's desk.

COMMITTEE CHAIR
...and we would have never even known that this was
happening if not for these boys' excellent report!

The Mayor looks at the boys, who stand
with their arms behind their backs.

MAYOR
You're telling me that students from Mr. Garrison's
class actually did something that had some
kind of relevance to the world?

COMMITTEE CHAIR
That's right.

Mr. Garrison smiles.

MAYOR
Mr. Garrison... The guy with the puppet.

COMMITTEE CHAIR
Yes.

MAYOR
Well, I must say, Garrison, perhaps you're not as stupid
and crazy as I always tell people you are.

MR. GARRISON
Thank you, Mayor. I don't want to
sound like a dickhole, but I...

COMMITTEE CHAIR
Mayor, these boys want that Harbucks
Coffee shut down! Right now!

COMMITTEE
YEAH!

The boys just stand there.

MAYOR
Well, I can't just shut them down. This is a free country.

COMMITTEE CHAIR
But they're ruining our city!

MAYOR
Look, the best I can do is create a proposition.
We'll call it Prop 10. The town can vote on it,
and if it passes... we'll see what we can do.

COMMITTEE
Hooray!

COMMITTEE CHAIR
What do you say boys?! We're gonna pass a law!

The boys just stand there. Finally Stan speaks.

STAN
Uh... hooray.

MAYOR
So I guess you want to do some campaigning.
You can do commercials and things like that.
We'll have a vote in the middle of town...
and obviously if more than 50% of the people...
While the Mayor rambles on the gnome music begins.
Tweek trys to figure out where the music is coming from.
His mouth drops when they come in singing and head
toward the Aide's leg. The gnomes crawl up his leg
and steal his underpants off his body.

TWEEK
AGH!!

The gnome on the Aide's leg throws the underpants
down to other gnomes and they walk off.

MAYOR
...want Harbucks out, then they're out.
So good luck to you.

Everyone but Tweek turns to go.
Tweek just stands there and points.

TWEEK
DIDN'T YOU SEE THEM?!

MAYOR
Alright, what's next?

AIDE
Next is issue #37-D Missing Underpants...

AIDE 2
Is it cold in here?

MR. GARRISON
Oh boys, could I have a quick this n' that with you?

The boys walk over to Garrison.

MR. GARRISON
Boys, I don't know who wrote that report, but now that
you've convinced everybody, you better stick with it.
Because if these people find out you didn't really write
that paper, and I actually do get fired, then Mr. Hat
is going to do horrible things to you.

Mr. Hat whispers in Garrison's ear.

MR. GARRISON (cont'd)
Oh, not THAT, MR. HAT! That's REALLY HORRIBLE!!
(To boys)
Anyway, good luck passing your new law.

Garrison leaves.

TWEEK
Jesus, man! Jesus! What are we gonna do?! HUH?!

INT. T.V. STUDIO - DAY

ANNOUNCER
Live, it's the South Park Town Hall Meeting on
Public Access. Tonight's topic - Prop 10!

A TV host is standing behind the podium with Postum
on his right and the boys on his left.

T.V. HOST
Should Harbucks be allowed to open a store in
South Park? That's tonight's topic.

Now we see the large audience. They all applaud.

T.V. HOST (cont'd)
On my left, five innocent, starry-eyed boys
from middle America. On my right, a big fat
smelly corporate guy from New York.

The audience all BOOS.

MR. POSTUM
Hey, I'm not fat or smelly!

T.V. HOST
Alright, Mr. Douche bag-

MR. POSTUM
Postum!

T.V. HOST
Oh, pardon me, Mr. Assface. Anyway,
let's hear your side of the argument.

CROWD MEMBER
BOO!

MR. POSTUM
My argument is simple. This country is founded on free
enterprise. Harbucks is an organization that -

(As the crowd gets louder and louder, booing,
Postum also goes up and up in volume)

Mr. Tweek, who is standing next to his
wife by the audience, looks at his wife
and smiles. She doesn't smile back.

MR. POSTUM
- AN ORGANIZATION THAT PRIDES ITSELF ON GREAT COFFEE.
WE SIMPLY WANT TO - AW TO HELL WITH YOU!!

(Finally the booing gets so loud
that Postum is inaudible. He stops)

T.V. HOST
Okay uck-up-fay, now for the other side of the argument,
we turn to our young, handsome lads.

Everything gets silent as the spotlight turns to the boys.

They look like deer caught in headlights.

T.V. HOST (cont'd)
Boys, your thoughts?

The boys say nothing.

Finally, Tweek starts smashing his head into his chair.

T.V. HOST (cont'd)
Come on boys... Don't be shy.
What's your principal argument?

Stan and Kyle look at each other. Then at Mr. Garrison,
who is standing in the wings. Garrison folds his arms
and looks sternly at the boys.

KYLE
Uh...

STAN
Uh...

CARTMAN
(Pointing at Postum)
This guy sucks ass!

The audience erupts into cheers and applause.

T.V. HOST
Great argument! You win, boys!

MR. POSTUM
WHAT?!

In the wings, Mr. Garrison wipes sweat
off his forehead and sighs relief.

MR. GARRISON
That was close, Mr. Hat.

INT. T.V. SET - DAY

This is a commercial on a television.

The screen is black, as slow, patriotic music
(Glory, glory hallelujah) starts to play.

FADE UP on an American flag.

ANNOUNCER
What is the future of America? Is it the money we make?
The quests we conquer? No. It's children...

Slowly, Kyle's head dissolves in frame. It moves
slowly from bottom of frame to top.

ANNOUNCER (cont'd)
So what do children say about Prop 10?

All the boys' faces drift through frame, and we
hear their voices as they do (not lip-synced).

KYLE (V.O.)
I don't like big corporations.

STAN (V.O.)
I like small businesses.

CARTMAN
I believe in the family-owned business.

KENNY
Mph rmph rm rmphm rm.

TWEEK
AGH!

ANNOUNCER
It's time to stop large corporations. Prop 10 is about
children. Vote yes on Prop 10, or else... You hate
children. You don't hate children, do you?

The American flag comes back in the background
as all the boys' faces settle in the frame.

ANNOUNCER (cont'd)
Remember... keep American business small or else...

A graphic image of the boys' heads being burned.

ANNOUNCER (cont'd)
Paid for by Citizens for a Fair and Equal Way to get
Harbucks Coffee Kicked Out of Town Forever.

(CHYRON: CITIZENS FOR A FAIR AND EQUAL WAY TO GET
HARBUCKS COFFEE KICKED OUT OF TOWN)

INT. SOUTH PARK COMMITTEE ROOM - DAY

The Committee is gathered around a T.V. watching this ad.
The Committee woman snaps it off.

COMMITTEE CHAIR
Well? What do you think?

MR. TWEEK
Wow! It's great!

COMMITTEE CHAIR
Yes it is! We'll put it on the air immediately!

MR. TWEEK
(To Mrs. Tweek)
What do you think, hon? Hon?

Mrs. Tweek folds her arms and walks away.

MR. TWEEK (cont'd)
(Following her)
What's the matter?

MRS. TWEEK
I have a big problem with this.

MR. TWEEK
What do you mean?

MRS. TWEEK
We're just using those boys for our benefit.
They have no idea what they're saying.

MR. TWEEK
But kids are great to get people on our side.

MRS. TWEEK
You don't just throw a child in a political commercial to
sell your beliefs. I won't be a part of this anymore!

She leaves.

MR. TWEEK
Honey, all's fair in love and war... and coffee... Hon.

EXT. HARBUCKS COFFEE

Protestors are out front with signs like
'SAY NO TO CORPORATE COFFEE!'

PROTESTOR
Take your corporate coffee and go back to New York City!

CROWD
YEAH!

PROTESTOR 2
It's people like you who are ruining Main Street USA!

CROWD
YEAH!

The protestors are in a frenzy.

PROTESTOR 2
How many Native Americans did you
slaughter to make that coffee huh?!

The crowd pauses.

CROWD
YEAH!!!

MR. POSTUM
Damn, these people aren't buying any coffee.
I'll have to try and appeal to the younger crowd.

EXT. HARBUCKS COFFEE

Mr. Postum stands outside the Harbucks coffee
store dressed as a big cartoonish camel carrying
a bunch of kiddiechinos.

The protestors are there, the customers are there.
It's like a circus.

CAMEL JO
Hey kids! I'm Camel Joe and I love a fresh cup of coffee!
It's yummdilliscious! And it makes you feel SUPER!

The kid doesn't respond.

CAMEL JO
(Pulls out a colorful mug)
I have a surprise for you! The new 'Kiddiechino' from
Harbucks! More sugar and all the other goodies kids
like with all the caffiene of a normal double latte!

MOTHER
No Billy! No coffee for you!
(To Mr. Harbucks)
You should be ashamed of yourself!
Using cartoons to push caffeine on children!

MR. POSTUM
Why don't you go back to the hole you
crawled out from lady!

MR. TWEEK
Mr. Postum, I'm afraid you've got a
lot to learn about making coffee.

MR. POSTUM
Oh, and you don't. Your coffee tastes
like three day old moldy diarhea.

MR. TWEEK
Well, I'm sorry to inform you that this town
is having a vote tomorrow, and if the law
passes you're gonna be thrown out of town.

MR. POSTUM
What!

MR. TWEEK
At five o'clock, the best coffee wins, either your
coffee... or a fresh warm cup of Tweek's coffee, like an
old sweater that keeps getting warmer with age, you can
count on Tweek's coffee to start your day!

Mr. Tweek tips his hat and walks away.

Meanwhile, the Mayor is with her two aides and the South
Park Committee in front of the two coffee houses.

As she talks, she walks around and
points out where things will be, and
the two aides follow her like puppies.

MAYOR
Tomorrow for the prop 10 vote we'll
set up ballot booths... here.

The aides take notes.

MAYOR
Alright, then we'll throw up the stage here. Before the
vote we'll get a band everyone likes... like, uh, like...

AIDE
Toto.

MAYOR
Like Toto. And then the Harbucks guy will have
five minutes to speak and the boys will have
five minutes to speak and then the town votes!

Garrison and the boys are standing off
to the side hearing all this.

MR. GARRISON
Uh, boys, you better get your asses to work.

CARTMAN
What now?

MR. GARRISON
They're expecting you to give a big speech on corporate
takeovers and this time it has to last five minutes.

KYLE
Oh, God! When is this gonna end!

STAN
Your dad really screwed us, Tweek!

TWEEK
Jesus, dude! I'm to blame for all this!
I'm to blame for everything!

INT. TWEEKS HOUSE - NIGHT

The boys are in Tweek's room again with cups of coffee.

Kyle is sitting on the bed with a notepad and a pen.

KYLE
So what are we gonna say?

CARTMAN
Why can't we just read the paper we wrote last time?

STAN
Cuz' then they'll know we didn't write
it, dummy! We have to be original!

KYLE
Does anybody know anything about corporations?

Meanwhile, Tweek looks over and
sees the gnomes walk in again.

TWEEK
WAGH!

CARTMAN
I think my mom is a corporation.

STAN
Yeah. That makes sense.

TWEEK
YOU GUYS! SHH!!

The gnomes walk in and get in Tweek's underwear drawer.

KYLE
Well how about we just say corporate should be stopped.

STAN
How do we stretch that into five minutes?

TWEEK
THEY'RE TAKING MY UNDERPANTS!!!

KYLE
Will you stop with the underpants
gnomes, Tweek?! We have to WORK here!

Tweek says nothing. He just points to his dresser
where the underpants gnomes are standing.

STAN
What the hell?!

CARTMAN
Well, I'll be damned...

                    TWEEK
        That's my last pair of underpants!

        The boys run over to the gnomes.
        All but one of them run away.
    The defiant one just stands there and looks nervous.

                    KYLE
            Shh! Don't scare him!

                    STAN
            Hey there, little guy.

    Cartman WHACKS the little gnome with a stick.

                    CARTMAN
                    BAD!

                    KYLE
                Cartman!

                    CARTMAN
                What?!

                    KYLE
    Why do you always have to hit stuff with a stick?!

                    CARTMAN
    Well look at him! He's all... you know... look at him.

            He hits him again.

                    GNOME
            Is that you got pussy?

                    CARTMAN
                    WHAT?!

                    STAN
                Hey, he talked!

                    CARTMAN
    Yeah, he called me a pussy. I'm not a pussy YOU'RE a pussy!

                    GNOME
            YOU'RE a pussy, PUSSY!

                    CARTMAN
                    AY!

                    STAN
    Dude, why are you taking Tweek's underpants?

                    KYLE
    Yeah, look what you're doing to this poor kid!

                    TWEEK
                    AGH!

GNOME
Stealing underpants big business!

STAN
Business? Wait, do you know anything about business?

GNOME
Sure! That's what gnomes do!

KYLE
Show us!

GNOME
Okay, follow me!

The gnome walks out. The boys follow him.

CARTMAN
Little pussy gnome! Don't call ME a pussy! Pussy gnome.

EXT. SOUTH PARK - NIGHT

Silhouette shot of the gnome leading the boys through some trees. The moon and stars fill the sky.

**Note - none of the following has to be lip-synced since it will all be silhouetted.

GNOME
Not much longer now!

CARTMAN
Are you taking us to your little pussy house?

GNOME
No, pussy, I'm taking you to my village.

CARTMAN
Oh, your pussy village?

KYLE
Cartman will you just shut up and let him show us!

Now, in a non-silhouetted shot, they come to a tree. The gnome knocks on it three times and a little door opens.

GNOME
Follow me!

CARTMAN
I hope we're not wasting our time with this little pecker.

EXT. SOUTH PARK AVENUE - DAY

Postum is standing outside his Harbucks, looking for customers.

MR. POSTUM
Well... It looks like Harbucks will never make
it in this town... Alright, boys that's it!

Postum turns to the workers still
working on the Harbucks.

MR. POSTUM
Pack it up! We're moving out of town.

WORKER
Aw, but we just finished!

MR. POSTUM
I know. But these folks obviously don't want us here.

WORKER #2
But what will become of us?

MR. POSTUM
Oh, quit being so melodramatic, Sanchez, Jesus Christ.

INT. GNOME CAVE - NIGHT

The boys follow the gnome into a huge cavern,
where hundreds of gnomes are hard at work.

In the middle of the cave is
a GIGANTIC pile of underpants.

The gnomes are all singing their gay little work song.

STAN
Damn, dude, this place is huge!

KYLE
Yeah, it's almost as big as Cartman's ass.

CARTMAN
No it isn't, you guys.

GNOME 1
This is where all our work is done!

KYLE
So what are you going to do with all
these underpants that you steal?

GNOME #1
Collecting underpants is just phase one.
Phase one, collect underpants.

KYLE
So, what's phase two?

The gnome sits there and thinks.
For a long time.

GNOMES

GNOME #1
(Calling out)
Hey... What's phase two?

Another gnome walks over.

GNOME #2
Phase one, we collect underpants.

GNOME #1
Yeah, yeah, yeah, what about phase two?

Gnome #2 thinks.

GNOME #2
Well... Phase THREE is Profit! Get it?

STAN
I don't get it.

The gnome walks over to another large sign. It has
colomns for phase one, phase two and phase three. Under
phase one it says 'Steal Underpants.' Under phase two it
says '?' And under phase three it says 'Profit.'

GNOME #2
You see? Phase one, collect underpants.
Phase two... ... ... Phase three, PROFIT!!

CARTMAN
Oh I get it.

STAN
No you don't, fat ass!

KYLE
Do you know guys anything about corporations?

GNOME #1
YOU BET WE DO!

The boys light up.

GNOME #2
Us gnomes are geniouses at corporations!

Above the boys, a group of gnomes are pushing
a large mine cart filled with underpants.
It slips off the track.

GNOME #4
JESUS CHRIST LOOK OUT!!

The cart falls on top of Kenny killing him instantly.

STAN
(Nonchalant)
Oh my God, they killed Kenny.

KYLE
You bastards. Listen, we have to give a huge speech
tomorrow about corporate takeovers.

GNOME
Holy shit! We killed your friend!

STAN
Yeah, yeah, yeah. Look, we've got to know about
corporate takeovers or tomorrow we're screwed.

GNOME
CHRIST! WE SQUISHED HIM LIKE A BUG!!

STAN
Do you anything about corporate takeovers?

GNOME #1
Well, we can explain that to you easily!

GNOME #2
Yes! For a price...

KYLE
What?

GNOME #1
You know.

STAN
Underpants?

Now all the gnomes in the cave cheer out.

GNOMES
UNDERPANTS!!!!!!!!

EXT. SOUTH PARK AVENUE - DAY

The masses have gathered in front of Tweek's
and Harbucks coffee. A little stage
has been set up between the two.

A band just finishes playing.

COMMITTEE CHAIR
Toto, ladies and gentlemen!

One guy claps and jumps up and down enthusiastically.
The rest just stand there.

GUY
YEAH! TOTO!! WOOO!! TO-TOHHH!!!

Most people have signs that say
'YES ON PROP 10!' and stuff.

COMMITTEE CHAIR
Alright, and now before we all vote Yes on prop 10, here
to remind us why, are the lovable, innocent children.

The crowd goes wild as the boys take the stage.

Stan walks up to the mic and clears his throat.

STAN
Uh... Since we are so concerned with the corporate
takeovers, we went and asked our friends the underpants
gnomes, and they told us all about big corporations...

Kyle walks up to the mike.

CROWD MEMBER
Underpants gnomes?

KYLE
Big corporations are good!

CROWD MEMBER
What, good?

KYLE
Because without big corporations we wouldn't have things
like cars and computers and canned soup.

And then -

STAN
Even Harbucks coffee started off as a small little
business. But because it made such great coffee, and
because they ran their business so well, they managed to
grow and grow until it became the corporate powerhouse it
is today. And that is why we should let Harbucks stay!

Stan throws his arm in the air with a smile.

But nobody else smiles. They are silent.

COMMITTEE CHAIR
That's not what you said last time!

KYLE
Oh. Uh... Well the truth is we didn't
write that paper last time.

The townspeople are all stunned.

Way in the background, we can hear Garrison screaming.

MR. GARRISON
You little turd! You ruined my life for the last time!!

Garrison gets hauled off (still in the very wide shot)

Finally, Tweek's mom starts to applaud.

Everyone turns and looks at her.

She gets up on stage with the boys.

MRS. TWEEK
These boys are absolutely right! We've been using these
poor kids to pull at your heartstrings for our cause and
it's wrong. We're as low and despicable as Rob Reiner.

The crowd is silent.

MRS. TWEEK
You keep protesting and complaining, but did any
of you ever even bother to TASTE Harbucks coffee?

Everyone looks at each other.

MRS. TWEEK
Harbucks coffee got to where it is by being the best.
Don't you think you should at least try it?

In a mob, all together, the crowd
walks over to the Harbucks.

One by one, Postum starts handing out coffees.

COMMITTEE MEMBER
Hey! This is pretty damn good!

COMMITTEE MEMBER #2
Yeah, it doesn't have that bland, raw sewage
taste that Tweek's coffee has...

Now even Mr. Tweek walks over and tastes Postum's coffee.

MR. TWEEK
Hey... Hey that IS good!

MR. POSTUM
It's a French Roast.

MR. TWEEK
It's subtle and mild. Mild like that first splash
of sun on an April morning. This coffee is
coffee the way it should be -

Now everyone gathers around and
drinks the Harbucks coffee.

MR. POSTUM
Hey, no hard feelings Tweek. You know, we still
need someone to RUN this Harbucks coffee house.
I'm sure it will make a lot of money.

MR. TWEEK
Thank you, Mr. Postum. But I think we'll be fine with
the money we make selling our son into slavery.

GNOMES

TWEEK
AGHGH!!

MR. TWEEK
Just kidding son!

Everyone laughs merrily.

CARTMAN
I love you guys!

EPISODE 301
RAINFOREST
SCHMAINFOREST

BY MATT STONE & TREY PARKER

INT. SCHOOL - DAY

MR. GARRISON
Okay, children we have a special guest today.
A woman recruiting young people
for a national choir tour.

MRS. STEVENS, the choir teacher, steps in with a
group of kids with 'G.G.W.K.' sweatshirts on.

MR. GARRISON
Now, I know that choir tours
are totally stupid and lame,
but PLEASE give her your full attention.
(To choir teacher)
Go ahead.

The choir teacher looks at Mr. Garrison oddly,
and then steps in front of him.

CHOIR TEACHER
Uh, thank you... Mr. Garrison.
HOW ARE WE ALL DOING TODAY?!

No response.

CHOIR TEACHER (cont'd)
I CAN'T HEAR YOU! I SAID HOW ARE WE ALL DOING?!

Silence. Cartman farts.

MR. GARRISON
ERIC CARTMAN, YOU SAY EXCUSE ME!!

CARTMAN
Okay.

MR. GARRISON
Go ahead.

CHOIR TEACHER (cont'd)
Children, we are a national choir called
'Getting Gay With Kids!!' We're gonna do a BIG
tour down in Central America to help Save the
Rainforest and YOU CAN BE A PART OF IT!!

Nobody looks interested.

KENNY
Mph rmph rm.

The boys LAUGH.

MR. GARRISON
KENNY McKORMICK YOU SPEAK WHEN
YOU'RE SPOKEN TO!! Go ahead.

                    CHOIR TEACHER
You see, we take kids from all over the country, and put
    them in a choir where we sing and dance to raise
      awareness about our vanishing rainforests!

        An ugly boy with glasses steps forward.

                      UGLY BOY
      Did you know over ten thousand acres of
        rainforest are bulldozed every year?

      Now a cute little blonde girl steps forward.
              (Her name is KELLY)

                       KELLY
    That's right. And over thirty percent of the
      world's oxygen is made in the rainforest!

      Kenny's eyes grow wide. He is in love.
  Kelly smiles back at Kenny. Kenny's eyes get droopy.

                    CHOIR TEACHER
          So who wants to join the fun?!

                     CARTMAN
          What if you have no rhythm?

                    CHOIR TEACHER
                  Excuse me?

                     CARTMAN
      Like my friend Kyle, he Jewish,
        so he doesn't have any rhythm.

                       KYLE
              Shut up, fat ass!!

                       STAN
                  Choirs suck.

                    MR. GARRISON
        KYLE BROFLOSKI YOU WATCH YOUR LANGUAGE!
    ERIC CARTMAN YOU BE NICE TO PEOPLE, STAN MARSH YOU
  MIND YOUR MANNERS! KENNY MCKORMICK YOU PAY ATTENTION!
                (To choir teacher)
                  Go ahead.

    The choir teacher is amazed by Garrison's ability.

                    CHOIR TEACHER
          Well, uh that's all, really -

    Kenny and the little girl exchange looks again.
      This time, the little girl picks her nose.

      - So, if anyone is interested in seeing the
    rainforest and joining our choir, I'll leave
          information packets up front.

CARTMAN
That's good, we need some more toilet paper.

MR. GARRISON
ALRIGHT, THAT DOES IT!!

INT. COUNSELOR'S OFFICE - DAY

You know that kid that we always see in front
of the Counselor's office, and the Principal's office?
Well, his name is CRAIG. And now he is sitting
opposite Mr. Mackey being scolded.

MR. MACKEY
I'm tired of seeing you in my office, young man.
You get sent here every day, Craig!

CRAIG
I know.

MR. MACKEY
Why can't you behave?

CRAIG
I don't know.

MR. MACKEY
What do you have to say for yourself?
(beat)
Well I tell you what, young man, you're gonna
be held back a grade if you don't -

Craig flips him off.

MR. MACKEY
Did you just flip me off?!

CRAIG
No.

MR. MACKEY
Yes you did! You just flipped me the bird! Now see,
that is exactly what I'm talking about. If you don't
shape up, mkay, and get your head straight -

Craig lifts his middle finger again.

MR. MACKEY
THERE! YOU FLIPPED ME OFF AGAIN!

CRAIG
No I didn't.

MR. MACKEY
Yes you did! And until you stop flipping
people off you can just go back to the
waiting room, mkay! NEXT!

Craig gets up just as the door opens
and our four boys walk in.

MR. MACKEY
Well, well, well, mkay, if it isn't Stan,
Kyle, Kenny and Eric.

KYLE
Hey, Craig.

(We can't see Craig as he walks out, his back is to us.)

CARTMAN
HEY! Don't flip me off, you son of a bitch!

MR. MACKEY
Sit down, boys. Now let's see what did
Mr. Garrison send YOU in here for?

Mackey reads over a piece of paper.

MR. MACKEY
'The boys were being rude while a choir teacher
was giving some stupid presentation.'

STAN
It just some dumb activist kids' choir thing.

MR. MACKEY
Uh, young man, Getting Gay With Kids is not dumb, mkay.
It just so happens that I am on the board of directors!

KYLE
Dude, all those choirs are the same. They don't even
really sing, they use pre-recorded tapes!

MR. MACKEY
Well guess what, boys? I think that
Getting Gay With Kids is just what you need.
I'm going to sign up all four of you.

STAN
What?!

KYLE
You can't do that!

KENNY
Woo-hoo!!

The other boys look at Kenny oddly.
Kenny quickly lowers his arms
and tries to look bummed.

KENNY
(muffled, of course)
I mean... Aw!

MR. MACKEY
I think this will be very good for you.

STAN
But we don't even CARE about the rainforest!

MR. MACKEY
And that's exactly why you need to go, mkay.

CARTMAN
(On his knees)
Please, Mr. Mackey, we'll be good! Don't send us to
that ol' kids' choir! Have mercy, Mr. Mackey!

EXT. CARTMAN'S HOUSE - DAY

The boys' mothers are loading their kids into the big
Getting Gay With Kids bus. The choir teacher stands
at the bus door, holding a clipboard.

KYLE'S MOTHER
Be safe, Kyle. Bring me something back
from the rainforest.

CHOIR TEACHER
Oh, no, no, no. The rainforest is very fragile.
We must take only pictures and leave only footprints.

KYLE'S MOTHER
Oh, I didn't realize.

ODD KID
(Out the bus window)
Did you know that right now, bulldozers are tearing
down thousands of acres of rainforest every day?

CARTMAN
Aw, man, this is gonna suck donkey balls.

Stan's mother is dragging Stan by the arm towards the
big Getting Gay With Kids bus.

STAN
Please don't make me go on a choir tour, mom! PLEASE!

STAN'S MOTHER
Stan, you should be excited! I would love to see the
rainforest. Besides, your dad and I need some time alone.

STAN
Noooooo!

Stan's mother pitches him into the bus
like a load of laundry.

The doors close and the bus heads away.

INT. BUS - DAY

The choir teacher stands at the front of the bus.

CHOIR TEACHER
Okay children, that's all of us! We're ready to
head for the Latin American nation of Costa Rica,
a country filled with virgin rainforest.

CARTMAN
Whoopee.

CHOIR TEACHER
And you must be Eric Cartman. I heard about you.
You don't respect nature or other cultures.

CARTMAN
Yeah, pretty much.

CHOIR TEACHER
Well, I'm gonna change the way you think, kiddo.

Kenny sits down right next to the little blonde girl.
They look at each other while sweet music plays.
Finally, the little girl speaks.

LITTLE BLONDE GIRL
My name's Kelly.

KENNY
Mph rm rmhpm.

LITTLE BLONDE GIRL
Lenny?

KENNY
Mph, RMHPM.

LITTLE BLONDE GIRL
Johnny?

KENNY
RMHPM!!!
LITTLE BLONDE GIRL
(Picking her nose)
Oh.

CHOIR TEACHER (cont'd)
Now we've got a LONG trip ahead of us, so let's take
the opportunity to learn our choreography!

CARTMAN
The nightmare begins...

EXT. BUS - DAY

The bus travels south down to Latin America.

INT. BUS - DAY

The bus drives on.

CHOIR TEACHER
Oh look, children! I think we're entering San José,
which is the capital of Costa Rica!

The kids all look out their windows.

CHOIR TEACHER (cont'd)
Oh, this is so exciting!

CARTMAN
Oh my God, dude, look how dirty and
crappy everything is!

CHOIR TEACHER
Eric, Costa Rica is a third world country.
These people are much poorer than those in the U.S.

CARTMAN
Well why they hell don't they get jobs?

EXT. BUS - DAY

As the bus drives through the poorest part of town,
Cartman sticks his head out the window.

CARTMAN
AY! Why don't you people quit slacking
off and get a job?! What's wrong
with you?! Go to college!!

INT. BUS - DAY

CHOIR TEACHER
Eric, sit down!

CARTMAN
Look, you gotta be firm with these people or they'll
slack off and be poor forever. Right, Kenny?

Kenny glares at Cartman.

CARTMAN
Hey maybe that's it, Kenny. Maybe you're Costa Rican
and that's why your family is so poor!

Kenny looks at Kelly, worried about what she thinks.

KENNY
Mph rmph rm.

KELLY
Your family ISN'T poor?

Kelly goes back to picking her nose.

CARTMAN
Whoa, dude! Look over there!!

EXT. BUS - DAY

Three scantily dressed Costa Rican WOMEN are on the
street corner waving to cars that drive by.

INT. BUS - DAY

CARTMAN
Wow! Costa Rican prostitutes!
Hey look at the prostitutes, you guys!

The prostitutes notice Cartman staring
at them, and get angry.

PROSTITUTE
(Thick accent)
What are Jew looking at, main?!

PROSTITUTE 2
(thick accent)
Hey, why don't you take a picture?

Cartman holds up his empty hands to eyes.

CARTMAN
(thick accent)
Okay, cleeeeeek!

CHOIR TEACHER
Eric! Sit down!

EXT. SAN JOSÉ NATIONAL HALL - DAY

The bus pulls up to the National Hall
and the kids all pour out.

CHOIR TEACHER
Kids, this is the Costa Rican Capital building!
This is where all the leaders of the
Costa Rican Government make their-

CARTMAN
Oh God it smells like ass out here!

CHOIR TEACHER
Alright, that does it!

The choir teacher grabs Cartman's arm and
leans down in his face.

CHOIR TEACHER (cont'd)
Eric Cartman you respect other cultures THIS INSTANT!

CARTMAN
I wasn't saying anything about their culture,

I was just saying their city smells like ass.

Meanwhile, Kenny and Kelly are standing off to the side.

KELLY
Wow... Seeing a place like this really makes you
appreciate living in America, huh?

KENNY
(Dreamy-eyed)
Mph-hm.

Kelly picks her nose.

CHOIR TEACHER
(Continuing)
You may think that making fun of third
world countries is funny, but let me-

CARTMAN
I don't think it's funny! This place is overcrowded,
smelly and poor - that's not funny, that sucks!

The Choir Teacher sighs.

CHOIR TEACHER
Eric, will you please, PLEASE, just keep your mouth shut
while we present ourselves to the Costa Rican President?

CARTMAN
Why?

CHOIR TEACHER
(Out the side of her mouth)
Because I'll buy you some ice cream afterwards if you do.

CARTMAN
Eh-OH!

INT. SAN JOSÉ NATIONAL HALL - DAY

The kids are standing in a large hall
decorated with flags and pictures of Costa
Rican leaders. The choir teacher is standing
in front of them, talking right into camera-

CHOIR TEACHER
Well, it was a long trip, but the children are
VERY excited to sing tomorrow!

Now we see the reverse angle. A big Costa Rican
LEADER sits behind a crappy desk. And a few
other official looking Costa Ricans stand
beside him. They all look confused.

LEADER
Que?

CHOIR TEACHER
Uh... We're the choir... that was sent
from the United States.

LEADER
Que?

CHOIR TEACHER
We're the group singing for the Save the
Rainforest summit tomorrow? Oh dear, where is
Mr. Mackey he should have been here by now...

The Costa Ricans still just look confused.

CHOIR TEACHER (cont'd)
Children, do any of you speak Spanish?

The kids all just stand there and blink. Kelly picks
her nose. Finally, Cartman raises his hand.

CHOIR TEACHER (cont'd)
Don't you DARE.

Cartman slowly lowers his hand.
Just then, Mr. Mackey walks in.

MR. MACKEY
Sorry I'm late.

CHOIR TEACHER
Oh thank goodness you're here, I don't speak any Spanish.

MR. MACKEY
Oh, no problem.
(Talking to leader)
Uh ustedes choir de Estados Unidos, Mbien.
(We're the choir from the United States)

LEADER
Oh... Oh! Save Da Rainforest!

CHOIR TEACHER
Yes!

LEADER
Pablo los llevara en un tur de la jungla.
(Pablo will take you on a rainforest tour)

MR. MACKEY
Uh, he says Pablo here will take you on a rainforest tour.

The rainforest guide steps out and waves.

CHOIR TEACHER
Oh boy! Mr. Presidente, round up
all your subjects outside! We have a
special gift for you! The gift... Of song!

PRESIDENTE
Que?

EXT. SAN JOSÉ NATIONAL HALL - DAY

The kids are all gathered on the small square in front of
the old, dirty building. They absolutely sparkle in their
neat, Getting Gay With Kids shirts and white gloves.

CHOIR TEACHER
Alright children, let's get in our
rows quickly so we can begin!

STAN
I don't remember all the words!

CHOIR TEACHER
That's okay, just sing with the tape. Nobody will notice.

The kids get in their rows.

The Presidente and his people look confused.

KELLY
Did you remember all the choreography, Lenny?

KENNY
(I think so)
Rm rmph rm.

The choir teacher turns around and
addresses the poor Costa Ricans.

CHOIR TEACHER (cont'd)
Hello, everybody! This is just a little
rehearsal for tomorrow, so we may be a
little rusty, ha ha ha...

The choir teacher pulls a large boom box out of
nowhere and presses 'play.' Gay music begins.

KIDS
(Singing)
Doo Doo Doo Doo Doo. Zat A Doot A Waa.
There is a place that is magical and full of rain.
But now it needs help because it is in pain.
Cleaning the earth is a mighty big chore.
But we're spreading awareness like never before.

The poor Costa Ricans look on with confusion.

The choir teacher happily directs. She gestures
for the kids to put bigger smiles on their faces.

KIDS
(singing)
Getting Gay With Kids is here.
To spread the word and bring you cheer.

Let's save the rainforest. What do you
say? Being an activist is totally gay.

The kids all do a little choreography along with the
song. It's obvious that Kyle has no clue what is going on.

KIDS
(singing)
Someday if we work hard boys and girls,
there'll be nothing but rainforest
covering the entire world.
(beat)
Getting Gay With Kids is here.
To spread the word and bring you cheer.
Getting Gay With Kids is here.
So save the rainforest.
Totally gay. It's totally gay.

They finish with flourish but Kyle is still
out of sync with everybody else.

The Costa Ricans turn and go about their business
now that this distraction is over.

CHOIR TEACHER
Great job, gang!

She walks over to Kyle.

CHOIR TEACHER
You were really all over the place, Kyle.

KYLE
Thanks.

CARTMAN
I told you Jewish people don't have rhythm.

KYLE
FUCK OFF CARTMAN!!!

STAN
No, dude... I think Cartman might actually be right.

KYLE
No... Tha- That's a stereotype!

STAN
Dude... Maybe you really DON'T have any rhythm!

Kyle looks scared. Dramatic MUSIC STING.

ACT 2

INT. RAINFOREST - DAY

The group is hiking through dense rainforest,
led by the Costa Rican guide.

COSTA RICAN GUIDE
This is now secondary rainforest we are entering.
Notice the canopy of foliage.

CHOIR TEACHER
(Taking pictures)
Oh, it's everything I ever dreamed it would be!!

Stan steps very gingerly, as if walking
through a minefield. His eyes dart back
and forth in search of snakes.

STAN
AGH! SNAKE!

KYLE
No, dude, that's a branch.

STAN
Oh. AGH! SNAKE!

KYLE
No, that's that same branch again.

STAN
Oh.

COSTA RICAN GUIDE
The rainforest is very delicate and we
must take steps to protect it.

CARTMAN
Yeah, yeah, yeah, must take steps to protect it, bla bla bla.

The guide looks at Cartman oddly.

CARTMAN
We hear this a million times back up in the States.

The group journeys on.

COSTA RICAN GUIDE
Here look! These are squirrel monkeys!
Endangered inhabitants of rainforest.

As they walk by, a bunch of kids take
pictures of the bored-looking monkey.

KELLY
(Taking picture)
Wow, isn't he neat, Lenny?

Cartman picks up a stick and smacks it on the head.

CARTMAN
BAD! Bad monkey!

The monkey runs away.

165

CHOIR TEACHER
Eric, what the HECK are you doing?!

CARTMAN
I'm asserting myself. It's tough love. Just like my
Mr. Kitty. When he's bad I say 'That's a Bad Mr. Kitty!'
and I smack him on the head.

The choir teacher looks confused.

COSTA RICAN GUIDE
And here is a three-toed sloth.

Again, Cartman smacks it as he walks through.

CARTMAN
Bad! That's a BAD three-toed sloth!

The choir teacher grabs Eric and drags him away.

CHOIR TEACHER
ERIC FOR GOD'S SAKE KNOCK IT OFF!!

CARTMAN
(Still trying to hit him)
Respect my authority!

Now the group finally comes to a stop.

CHOIR TEACHER (cont'd)
Well, Mr. Pedro, this was a great tour,
but I guess we should be heading back.
We have a BIG concert tomorrow, don't we kids!

GAY KIDS
YEAH!

UGLY BOY
I wish we could have seen the Yanagopa!

KYLE
What's the Yanagopa?

CHOIR TEACHER
The Yanagopa are gentle, native people that live in the
rainforest. But bulldozers are destroying their home!
Soon they will have nowhere to go. So, we must stop
bulldozing the rainforest so that they can live -

CARTMAN
AGH GOD, here she goes AGAIN.

As he's saying this, Stan notices a medium-sized
snake moving slowly in a tree next to Kyle.

STAN
AAAGAHGHGHGAHAGHGHGHGHGH!!!!!!!!

CHOIR TEACHER
Stanly, what is it?!

STAN
SSSNNNAAAAKKKKEE!!!!!!

The kids all see the snake and gasp.
The guide very calmly walks over to it.

COSTA RICAN GUIDE
Oh yes, this is what we call a coral snake.
Notice his red markings. Quite an amazing creature.

STAN
AGAHGHAGHGH!!

COSTA RICAN GUIDE
What's the matter, little boy?

CARTMAN
He's a little wuss, what's it look like?

STAN
I'm just a-scared of snakes!

COSTA RICAN GUIDE
Now, now, you must remember; this snake is
more afraid of us than we are of it.

Just then, the snake violently and maliciously
leaps out at the guide, wraps around his neck,
and bites him on the head.

The kids watch in horror as the guide screams
and fights for his life. Stan runs screaming.

In seconds it's over, and the guide lies on
the ground, dead. The snake bites him a few
more times just to be more evil.

CHOIR TEACHER
OH MY GOD!!!

CARTMAN
Yeah, that snake is really scared of us alright.

CHOIR TEACHER
Jesus Christ, is he dead?!

STAN
DUDE!!!

KYLE
My guess would be yes.

CHOIR TEACHER
(Panicking)
Oh no! God no! Now don't panic children.

301

Scene 284 | Panel | BG

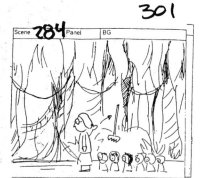

Location/Time

Dialogue
                    KYLE

              Kenny,

Action/Efx

        They all continue to walk.

Trans.

A3

287.01 Revisions 2/8/99   PAGE 126B

Scene 287.01 | Panel | BG

Location/Time

Dialogue
                    KYLE
         can I talk to you for a second?
Just friend to friend?

                    KENNY
Mph. Mph Mmphmmph?

                    KYLE
    Its this whole rhythm thing. My whole
life, I've never been bad at anything,
you know?

Trans.
        Kyle walks next to Kenny.

ALL KIDS WALK PAST
      THEM   133

288.01

Scene 288.01 | Panel | BG

UP WITH

Location/Time

Dialogue   KYLE
  I get straight A's in school,
I'm on the football team, I'm good at
everything I've ever tried. It's just
wierd to suck at something.

Action/Efx

Trans.

        109

Scene 289.01 | Panel | BG

Location/Time

Dialogue   KYLE
    How do you

    deal with it?

             KENNY

    Mph?

Acti   KYLE
  I mean, you suck at everything. You get
horrible grades, you can't do any sports
or anything. And you seem to deal with
it fine.

Trans.   Kenny thinks.

        13A

---

301 Revisions 2/8/99   PAGE 126C

Scene 289.02 | BG | S/A 288.01

UP WITH

Location/Time

Dialogue   KYLE
Yeah Maybe that's it. You just have to accept
   what you're bad at and move on. For
   someone like me, it's not having rhythm,
   and for someone like you, it's everything
   else. Yeah, now it makes sense.

Action/Efx

Trans.

        177

Scene 289.03 | BG | S/A 289.01

Location/Time

Dialogue   Kenny seems to agree.

                 KENNY

             Mph-mph.

 A Kyle let's out a sigh.

               KYLE
  Thanks Kenny. I feel a lot better after
getting that off my chest. Thanks.

                KENNY
  Mph.

* TD S/A 287.01 Delete
  OTher Kids
  (except Kny/Ky)   111

Cartman walks over to the snake with his stick.

CARTMAN
BAD! That's a BAD SNAKE!

Cartman whaps the snake, which immediately comes
charging after him-

CARTMAN
(Running away)
WAAGHGH!!

EXT. RAINFOREST - DUSK

The sun is starting to set as the choir teacher
leads her group around aimlessly.

CHOIR TEACHER
Maybe we came from that way...
No... No let's try this way.

KELLY
Benny, do you think we're gonna be okay?

KENNY
Mph. Mrph rm rphm.

KELLY
That's good... Can I tell you something?

KENNY
Mph.

KELLY
I think I like you.

KENNY
Mph?!

KELLY
Yeah. I mean, I think we communicate really well.

KENNY
Mph rm!!

KELLY
No, that's NOT good.

KENNY
Mph rm rmph?

KELLY
No! See, if I start to like you too much I'm only going
to get my heart broken. 'Cause we live on opposite
ends of the country. Once this choir tour is
over, we'll never see each other again -

Kelly starts to pick her nose. Kenny pulls her arm away.

KELLY
- and that would devastate me. So I can't have
feelings for you. I JUST CAN'T LENNY!!

Kelly melodramatically runs away.

KENNY
AW!

CHOIR TEACHER
Oh children, the sun is setting!
We have to find our way out of here QUICK!!

EXT. RAINFOREST - DUSK

Shot of the sun going down.

EXT. RAINFOREST - NIGHT

We can just see a silhouette of the rainforest and some
clouds moving through a starry sky.

There is some lightning, and thunder claps.

INT. RAINFOREST - NIGHT

This scene is pitch black the whole time, except for very
short bursts of visible animation when lightning strikes.

CHOIR TEACHER
Okay... Okay... Everything is just fine kids...
It's important that we all stick together.
Is everybody still here?

There is a long silence. Finally, one kid speaks up.

VOICE
I'm not.

CHOIR TEACHER
Who's not?

VOICE
Me.

Huge lightning, huge thunder.

KELLY
Benny, will you hold my hand?

Lightning flickers and we see Kenny take Kelly's hand.

KELLY
I don't want to get emotionally attached, though.

Lightning flashes again, and we see Kenny huddled
close to Kelly. Kelly is picking her nose.

                    STAN
OH MY GOD, DUDE!!! I just saw Tony Danza!

                CHOIR TEACHER
No you didn't just see Tony Danza, Stanly!

Lightning flashes and we see Tony Danza
    sitting next to the choir teacher.

EXT. RAINFOREST PEACE SUMMIT - DAY

Meanwhile, the Save The Rainforest Summit is happening
back in San José. It's a pretty big event. A large stage,
lots of banners, and little booths are set up everywhere.
    It's just as big, colorful and stupid as the
            Environmental Media Awards.

        The following is all done in Spanish,
            with English subtitles.

                  PRESIDENTE
        Bueno! Bueno! Pongan el arco iris al
            lado las tortugas muertas.
        (Good, good! Put the rainbow next to
        the picture of the dying sea turtles.)

            Mr. Mackey walks up.

                  MR. MACKEY
        Buenas Dias, Senior Presidente.
            (Hello, El Presidente.)

                  PRESIDENTE
        Que tal, esta todo bien?
    (Oh hello. Is everything going okay?)

                  MR. MACKEY
    Oh, muy bien... Senior Presidente, um,
        usted no ha visto el coro, no?
    (Oh fine, fine... You, uh, haven't
        seen the choir have you?)

                  PRESIDENTE
                    QUE!?
                   (WHAT?!)

                  MR. MACKEY
    Parece que anoche no regresaron al hotel, mbien.
(Well they never came back to the hotel last night...)

                  PRESIDENTE
        ESTA BROMEANDO MACKEY? MAS DE CIENMIL
        PERSONAS ATENDERAN ESTE EVENTO, Y ME DICE
        USTED QUE NO TENDRE A MIS CHIQUITOS LINDOS
            PARA QUE LES CANTEN? CONO! CARAJO!
        (YOU'VE GOT TO BE KIDDING!! I HAVE OVER A HUNDRED
    THOUSAND PEOPLE COMING TO THIS EVENT! ARE YOU TELLING
    ME I HAVE NO DARLING LITTLE KIDS TO SING TO THEM?!)

301   Act II pg. 17

Scene **178** | Panel | BG

Location/Time   EXT. FOREST - THE NEXT DAY

Dialogue

CHOIR TEACHER
(Worried)   OK (We're)

Action/Efx

The sun rises over the rainforest.

Trans.

58

SOUTH PARK

301   PAGE **81**

Scene **79** | Panel | BG

Location/Time

Dialogue
CHOIR TEACHER
We're going to find our way out of the rainforest and make it back for the concert in time.

CARTMAN
I told you the rainforest sucks ass, but did you listen? Noo-oooooo.

The group walks through the foliage.

Trans.   All in Normal Clothes. *NOT Walking   181

Scene **180** | Panel | BG

SHOT &
Dialogue
CUT

Location/Time

Dialogue   CHOIR TEACHER
We're going to find our way out of this rainforest.

Action/Efx

Trans.   Walking. (Track)   46

Scene **1800-1** | Panel | BG

SIDE Rev

Location/Time

Dialogue
CHOIR TEACHER
The rainforest is what keeps us alive, Eric! We're in a bit of a pickle right now but-

Action/Efx

Trans.

112

Scene **180.02** | BG SIA 192?

Eric

Side

Location/Time

Dialogue
CARTMAN
This is a pretty God damn big pickle!

Action/Efx

Trans.

44

PAGE **81 A**

Scene **180-03** | BG SIA 180.01

SIDE Rev

Location/Time

Dialogue
CHOIR TEACHER
Well, we just need to respect our mother rainforest and she will respect us.

Action/Efx

Trans.

104

MR. MACKEY
Estoy seguro que llegaran. No se preocupe olvidelo, mbien.
(I'm sure they'll get here...
No problem. Forget I said anything.)

EXT. FOREST - THE NEXT DAY

The sun rises over the rainforest.
The group walks through the foliage.

KYLE
Dude, we're totally lost. We're gonna die out here.

KELLY
We are?!

CHOIR TEACHER
Don't worry, Kelly, we're going to find our way
out of the rainforest and make it back for the
concert in time. We just need to respect our
mother rainforest and she will respect us.

KYLE
Mrs. Stevens, you have a bug on your back.

CHOIR TEACHER
Oh, really? Could you brush it off?

She turns around to REVEAL an absolutely huge,
horrifying bug that is actually half her
size clinging to her back.

BUG
ROAR!

KYLE
Umm, no.

Now Mrs. Stevens turns her head around to see the
enormity and horror of the bug.

CHOIR TEACHER
AGAHAGAH!!! OH MY GOD!!!

She jumps around like she's on fire.

CHOIR TEACHER (cont'd)
GET IT OFF A ME!!! FOR THE LOVE OF GOD!!
AAGAHAGHG!!! GET IT OFF A ME!!! OH MY GOD!!!

The kids eyes go back and forth like
they're watching a tennis match.
The Choir Teacher finally comes to a
stop and catches her breath.

CHOIR TEACHER (cont'd)
Okay... Children, we must understand that the insects of
the rainforest help the delicate balance of life here.

301 Revision
P 20

Scene **179.01** | Panel | BG

Location/Time

Dialogue

KYLE

Dude,

Action/Efx

TO use setup from 179
& make sure choir teacher
is facing same way as
this Board.

Trans.

X 24

SOUTH PARK 301 Revisions 3/8/99 PAGE 81 A 1

Scene **179.02** | Panel | BG

Location/Time

Dialogue

KYLE
we're totally lost. We're gonna
die out here.

Action/Efx

Trans.

X 49

Scene **179.03** | Panel | BG

Location/Time

Dialogue

CHOIR TEACHER
Don't worry, we're going to find our way
out of the rainforest and make it back
for the concert in time.

Action/Efx

Trans.

X 95

---

301 Revision
P 20

Scene **179.04** | Panel | BG

Location/Time

Dialogue

CARTMAN
Hey, maybe we'll end up on one of those
VH-1 Behind the music specials.

Action/Efx

Trans.

X 77

SOUTH PARK 301 Revisions 3/8/99 PAGE 81 A2

Scene **179.05** | Panel | BG

Location/Time

Dialogue

CHOIR TEACHER
Eric, hush.

Action/Efx

Trans.

X 22

Scene **179.06** | BG S/A 179.04

Location/Time

Dialogue

CARTMAN
'They were a choir who had it all... But
then... The bottom fell out of their
world, when Behind the Music Continues...

Action/Efx

Trans.

X 111

She turns to walk again and we see that the bug
is still in the exact same spot.

                    BUG
                    Roar.

              CHOIR TEACHER
          AGAHGAHG!!! OH MY GOD!!!

                    KYLE
      The rainforest sucks! I wanna go home!

                   KELLY
                   Me too!

EXT. FOREST - LATER

       The whole class is again walking through
        the rainforest. Everyone looks nervous.
      The kids are all MOANING and AD LIB COMPLAINING.

              CHOIR TEACHER
     Shh, children, let's try to listen to what the
       rainforest tells us. If we use our ears,
      she can tell us so many things, perhaps -

         Suddenly, Kyle runs SMACK into a
           guy in military fatigues.

                    KYLE
       AGAHGAHG!!!! THERE'S A DUDE HERE!!

          The choir teacher runs up.

              CHOIR TEACHER
        Oh thank goodness! Hello sir.
        We are lost. Can you help us?

                  SOLDIER
                   Que?

      Cartman pushes his way to the front.

                  CARTMAN
          Let me try, let me try-
             (speaking slowly)
     We are from America. A-MER-I-CA. We are lost and very
          hungry. Nesescito burreeeetos.

           He doesn't answer.

                    STAN
     I don't want a burrito. I want a taco. Supreme.

                  CARTMAN
          (motioning to his mouth)
                   TA-CO.

KYLE
I want two tostadas and mild sauce.

CARTMAN
Two ToSTAAA-DAs. And an EN-CHIR-EE-TO.

CHOIR TEACHER
Boys, please! Not every Spanish person eats
tacos and burritos. That's a stereotype.

He motions for them to follow.

CHOIR TEACHER
Children, he wants us to follow him! Oh thank goodness,
I think this ordeal is over!

EXT. MARXIST REBELS' CAMP.

They walk into a camp of Marxist rebels. A dozen or so
unsavory looking characters all with guns.

STAN
This doesn't look very safe.

KYLE
Yeah, I think we should get the hell out of here.

CHOIR TEACHER
Now, kids, let's be a bit more open-minded.
I've read all about this in Newsweek. This is a
'People's Army.' They are fighting the fascist
policies of their fascist government.

The choir teacher makes her way to a person that
appears to be the head of the group.

CHOIR TEACHER (cont'd)
Hello. Do you speak-a the English?

SUBCOMMANDER MARCOS
Who are you?

CHOIR TEACHER
Oh wonderful! We were lost and it's such a great
coincidence we found you! You see, we are here to protest
the government-sanctioned raping of your rainforest...

The military guys look unimpressed.

CHOIR TEACHER
(Theatrically)
We are fighters, just like you.
Could you help us get back to San José?

No response.

CHOIR TEACHER (cont'd)
Um... Oh I know! Perhaps you like a gift!

(Theatrical)
Well, we have only one gift to give. The gift... of song...

KIDS
AW!

She pulls her boombox out of nowhere and hits play.
Immediately the song starts.

KIDS
(Singing)
Doo Doo Doo Doo Doo. Zat A Doot A Waa.
There's a place that is magical, and full of rain!
But now it needs help because it is pain!

The choir teacher notices that again Kyle is off.
But this time, she panics.

CHOIR TEACHER
(Nervous, under her breath)
Kyle! For the love of GOD do the right choreography!

The choir teacher sneaks a look at the military guys.
They all look a little pissed.

CHOIR TEACHER (cont'd)
Oh Kyle, PLEASE!

But Kyle remains hopelessly off.

KIDS
(Singing)
Cleaning the earth is a mighty big chore.
But we're spreading awareness like never before.
Getting Gay With Kids is here!

SUBCOMMANDER MARCOS
ENOUGH!

The military guys are extremely unimpressed.

CHOIR TEACHER (cont'd)
Well we hope that our gift of
song has warmed your hearts...

SUBCOMMANDER MARCOS
We're not getting gay with any kids, okay.

CHOIR TEACHER
Uh, yeah... So... Do you have a phone we can use?

SUBCOMMANDER MARCOS
Yes, we have a phone. It's right over there
next to the 12-person jacuzzi.

He laughs. All the other soldiers start laughing too.

SUBCOMMANDER MARCOS
Now get out of here before we kill you.

The choir teacher thinks.

CHOIR TEACHER
If it's because of the little Jewish boy's choreography-

KYLE
HEY!

SUBCOMMANDER MARCOS
You white Americans make me sick. You waste food,
oil and everything else because you're so rich
and then you tell the rest of the world to save the
rainforest because you like its pretty flowers.

Suddenly, a shitload of GUNFIRE breaks out!

CHOIR TEACHER
AGH!

KIDS
AGH!

SUBCOMMANDER MARCOS
RAPIDO!! RAPIDO!!

The soldiers start firing their weapons all around them.
Everyone is running and shooting guns.

Kenny gallantly steps in front of Kelly, his arms
outstretched, protecting her from any bullets.

CHOIR TEACHER
Run children! Run!!!!

The choir teacher and kids all dash out of
frame as a couple EXPLOSIONS go off.

EXT. RAINFOREST PEACE SUMMIT - DAY

A huge crowd has shown up at the summit. The crowd is made
up of mostly American tourists and American celebrities.

Limos pull up.

PRESIDENTE
Donde putas esta al coro? El Espectaculo comienza pronto!
(Where the hell is our Choir?!
The show is supposed to start soon!)

MR. MACKEY
No se preocupe, El Presidente, estaran aqui.
Este evento es muy importante para que
la maestra del coro se lo pierda, mbien.
(Don't worry, El Presidente, they'll be here.
This is too important for the choir teacher to miss.)

EXT. FOREST - LATER

The group is walking along a river.

CHOIR TEACHER
HELLO?! ANYBODY?! HEEELLPP!!

A little kid, who is toward the front of the line
reaches out for a big, yellow flower.

KID
Wow, look at the pretty flower -

CHOIR TEACHER
Oh no no, Jake. That fragile flower
is very delicate, okay -

WHAM!!! The flower shuts on Clyde's
head like a Venus flytrap.

CLYDE
(muffled)
OH IT HURTS!! IT HURTS!!

CHOIR TEACHER
AGAAGHH!!!

The choir teacher runs over and tries to
pull out Clyde's flailing legs, but to no avail.
The flower swallows him up.

KELLY
(Crying)
Baha!!! I wanna go home!! I hate the rainforest!!

Kenny puts his arm around the little girl to console her.

KENNY
Mph rm. Rmph rm.

KELLY
Oh, Lenny, hold me.

Kenny holds her closer.

KELLY
(Pulling away)
No. I can't get attached.

She stands there for a minute.
And then goes back in his arms.

KELLY
Oh, but I do like you.

KENNY
Mph rm r -

KELLY
(Pulling away again)
Oh, but you're only going to leave me.

KENNY
(Frustrated)
Mph rm rmph rm!

EXT. SAVE THE RAINFOREST SUMMIT - DAY

NEWSREPORTER
We're here live in San José, Costa Rica, where hundreds
of rich Americans have gathered for the Save the
Rainforest summit. Everyone is here so that they can
feel good about themselves, and act like they aren't
the ones responsible for the rainforest's peril.

NEWSREPORTER 2
That's right, Bob. And of course the main attraction today
is the darling kids' choir 'Getting Gay With Kids.' All of
whom must be backstage preparing at this very moment...

EXT. RAINFOREST - DAY

The group continues on. Hopelessly lost.

CHOIR TEACHER
Oh there's just no END to this place!
I think maybe we're going in circles.
(Checking her watch)
Oh dear God! The summit starts in an hour!
I'm going to lose my job!

She turns her head and sees that same big bug on her back.

BUG
Roar.

CHOIR TEACHER
AGHAGAHGAH!!!!

She jumps and screams like before.

CARTMAN
This is bullcrap! I'm not following
this stupid hippie around anymore.

Carmtan starts to walk off.

CHOIR TEACHER
Eric, where are you going?

CARTMAN
I'm going this way!

CHOIR TEACHER
Young man, I am the adult here! And I say we go THIS WAY!

                    CARTMAN
Look, you can stay over m-hya, but I'M going over th-hya!

                 CHOIR TEACHER
        YOUNG MAN I HAVE HAD IT-

                    CARTMAN
        No, no, no, no - You m-hya. Me th-hya.
        Screw you guys... I'm going home.

            Cartman walks off.

                 CHOIR TEACHER
    GOOD! YOU DESERVE TO DIE YOU LITTLE BASTARD!!

In a WIDE SHOT, we see Cartman walk off one way and
    the rest of the class stay in the rainforest.

                 CHOIR TEACHER
        Eric we have to stay together!!

        We PAN along with Cartman.

He walks through the trees for a little bit -

                    CARTMAN
                (While he's walking)
        God damn stupid hippie activist! I should be
        at home nestled on the couch with my Mr. Kitty
        right now watching Fat Abbot cartoons -

He walks out into a working construction site.
Bulldozers go to and fro, dozens of workmen all around.

                    CARTMAN
            YES! I knew it! I'm saved!!!

            Cartman runs off.

EXT. RAINFOREST - DAY

        The choir teacher looks in the
        direction that Cartman went.

                    STAN
        Hey maybe Cartman was right.

                    KYLE
        Yeah, it happened once before.

                 CHOIR TEACHER
    No, the spirit of Maya has told me to go this way.

The class heads the other direction, into the forest.

EXT. CONSTRUCTION SITE

Cartman runs up to one of the workmen.

CARTMAN
Mister! You got to help me! I'm starving to death!

WORKMAN
What are you doing here little boy?

CARTMAN
I was with my class and we got all lost in the
rainforest and I need food! I'm fading fast!

WORKMAN
Lost in the rainforest?! Oh my lord!
Where are all the others?

CARTMAN
FOOD!! I HAVE TO HAVE FOOD!!!

Cartman falls on the ground melodramatically,
face down, arms splayed out.

WORKMAN
OH MY GOD! GET THIS CHILD SOME FOOD QUICK!!!

Cartman lifts up his head for a brief second.

CARTMAN
Chicken wings.

WORKMAN
Chicken wings!

Cartman lifts his head up again.

CARTMAN
Medium spicy.

EXT. RAINFOREST PEACE SUMMIT - DAY

The crowd has gotten very anxious.
They are all chanting.

CROWD
START THE SHOW! START THE SHOW! START THE SHOW!

Again, the following is in Spanish with subtitles.

PRESIDENTE
La gente esta anciosa. Dentro de poco
se alborotan y empiezan a tiran chochadas.
(The crowd is getting anxious.
They will start throwing things soon.)

MR. MACKEY
Estoy seguro que llegaran.
Solo un poquito mas de tiempo, mbien.
(I'm sure they'll be here. We just need a little more time.)

PRESIDENTE
Bueno, voy a entretenerlos con mis
chistes de polacos. Deseenme suerte.
(Well, I will try and amuse them with
my Pollock jokes. Wish me luck.)

MR. MACKEY
Mbien.
(Good.)

The Presedente takes the stage.
Everyone cheers and then quiets down.

PRESIDENTE
A cuantos polacos les toma comerse un burrito?
(How many Pollocks does it take to eat a burrito?)

Silence.

PRESIDENTE
Dos!
(Two!)

Silence.

PRESIDENTE
A cuantos polacos les toma manejar a Panama?
(How many Pollocks does it take to drive to Panama?)

EXT. RAINFOREST - DAY

The choir is still trudging through.

CHOIR TEACHER
OH GOD! This is a nightmare!
We're NEVER going to make the festival!

STAN
Hey look over there! Isn't that smoke?

Stan points to some smoke drifting over the trees.

CHOIR TEACHER
Let's go, quickly!

They all run.

EXT. FOREST CLEARING

They run into the clearing to find a small fire burning.

KYLE
Hey, it's a fire! That means there must be people!

There is a rustling in the bushes. And then they step
out, the little, three foot tall Yanagopa people.
They all carry spears and look ridiculous.

CHOIR TEACHER
Children! It's the Yanagopa!

The Yanagopa look nervous, but gather
in a circle around the group.

CHOIR TEACHER
Do not be afraid. We are not here to
tear down your rainforest...

YANAGOPA
Tom tilly ye?

CHOIR TEACHER
Look at how they live in peace with
all living things. Gentle, noble -

But even she knows how stupid she sounds.

CHOIR TEACHER
RUN FOR YOUR LIVES CHILDREN!!!

Just then, the tribesman all throw their
spears at once into the choir teacher's head.
She looks like a porcupine just got to her.

She stands there for a minute... Then -

CHOIR TEACHER
OW!

YANAGOPAS
(Chanting)
Tom tilly ye! Tom tilly ye! Tom tilly ye! Tom tilly ye!

STAN
Holy crap!

Everybody starts running. Yanagopas pursue
them with their spears. As the choir teacher runs,
the spears fall out of her head.

Kyle and Stan run through the
jungle as spears go flying by.

STAN
JESUS CHRIST!

CHOIR TEACHER
RUN RUN RUN!!!!

The choir teacher looks behind her and
again sees the same bug on her back.

BUG
Roar.

CHOIR TEACHER (cont'd)
AGHAGAHG!!!!!

She jumps until it flies away.

Kelly falls down!

KELLY
AAGH!!

The Yanagopa almost get to her, but Kenny
runs back into frame, picks her up and
carries her away as she picks her
nose.

KELLY
Benny!

The entire class runs headlong through a shallow
puddle. They immediately start sinking.

KYLE
What the hell!?

STAN
I'm sinking!!!

CHOIR TEACHER
It's quicksand!

The headhunters all stand around the quicksand
holding spears and poison dart guns ready.

They are trapped.

HEADHUNTERS
Tom tilly ye!

EXT. HEADHUNTERS VILLAGE - DAY

Random people's heads are on poles in the little village.

The children are sitting, alone, tied up around a fire.

STAN
All we ever heard about growing up was
'Save the Rainforest,' 'The Rainforest is Fragile...'

KYLE
Yeah. Fragile my ass.

KELLY
Larry, if we make it out of this, I want
to be your girlfriend. Even if we do live
in different places. I don't care.

KENNY
Mph rm rmph.

Kelly struggles to pick her nose,
but can't with her hands tied.

Ms. Stevens is tied up like Fay Rae in King Kong.
She is dressed in a cheerleader outfit.

                    CHOIR TEACHER
Okay... Just what the heck is going on here people?

The Yanagopa do a little dance around her.

                    YANAGOPA
Too la bil-le! Too la bil-le! Too la bil-le! Too la bil-le.

As they sing, a HUGE Yanagopa comes out. He is the size
of a small house, with a big fat belly.

                  GIANT YANAGOPA
                    (Super deep)
                    Tom Ti li ye!

                    CHOIR TEACHER
                    AAAGHGH!!!

                      KELLY
Oh no! That big thing is going to make
        love to Ms. Stevens!!

                    CHOIR TEACHER
ALRIGHT, THAT DOES IT!! GOD DAMN STUPID ASS RAINFOREST!!

The kids look surprised.

                    CHOIR TEACHER
THIS PLACE FUCKING SUCKS!! I WAS WRONG!!!
FUCK THE RAINFOREST!!! I FUCKING HATE IT!!!
        I FUCKING HATE IT!!!!!

                      STAN
Oh, now she figures it out.

WHHOOOOOSH!!! Suddenly, a huge bulldozer
comes flying through the trees. Driving it is
the workman from the construction site.

                     WORKMAN
Quick! Everybody help the children!

The headhunters all run away screaming
as the workmen run towards the kids.

The guy driving the bulldozer slams into two of the
headhunters, killing them both. Then he drives over some
snakes and that large bug for good measure.

                      STAN
Wow!

KYLE
Dude! Bulldozers RULE!!

WORKMAN
Come on! Let's get you back to civilization!!!

KIDS
Hooray!!!

CHOIR TEACHER
Hooray children!!

EXT. CONSTRUCTION SITE

The class and several workman are in the
construction site. The kids are all munching
down on hot dogs and everybody has some lemonade.

CHOIR TEACHER
How did you know where we were?

WORKMAN
Your little friend helped me out -

Cartman walks up.

CHOIR TEACHER
Eric?

CARTMAN
Who did you expect? Merv Griffin?

CHOIR TEACHER
What exactly are you guys doing out here with
all this construction equipment?

WORKMAN
We're clearing out big sections of the
rainforest for a lumber yard.

CHOIR TEACHER
Really? That's great!

WORKMAN
You mean, you don't mind?

CHOIR TEACHER
No! I hate the rainforest! You go right ahead
and plow down this whole fucking thing!

WORKMAN
That's swell!

KELLY
Okay, Benny, so in order for our long
distance relationship to work, we'll have
to call each other every other day.

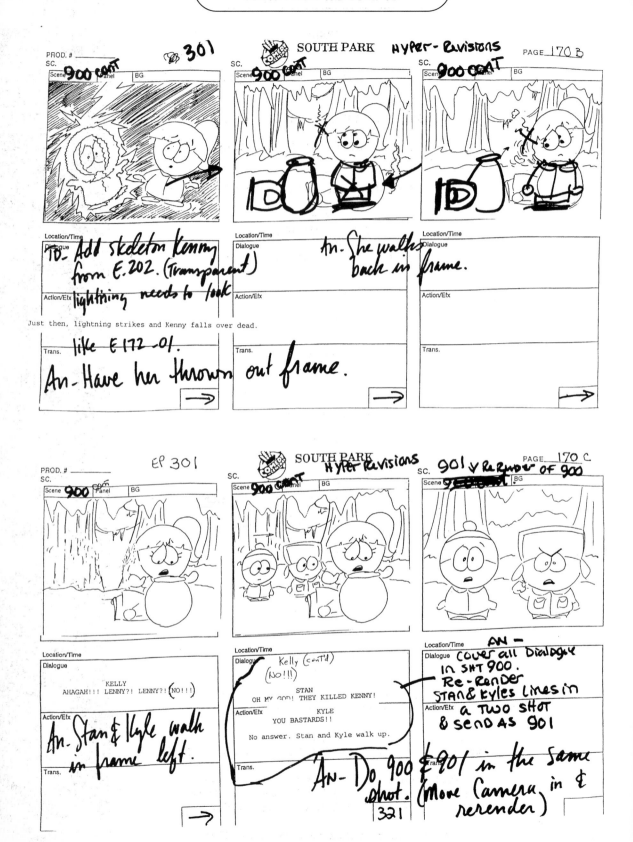

Just then, lightning strikes and Kenny falls over dead.

KELLY
AHAGAH!!! LENNY?! LENNY?! (NO!!!)

Kelly (cont'd)
(NO!!!)

STAN
OH MY GOD! THEY KILLED KENNY!

KYLE
YOU BASTARDS!!

No answer. Stan and Kyle walk up.

KENNY
Mph rm.

Just then, lightning strikes and Kenny falls over dead.

KELLY
AHAGAH!!! LENNY?! LENNY?! NO!!!

No answer. Stan and Kyle walk up.

STAN
OH MY GOD! THEY KILLED KENNY!

KYLE
YOU BASTARDS!!
KELLY
WHAT?! WHO?! WHO KILLED HIM?!

Stan and Kyle look confused.

STAN
THEY did.

KELLY
Who's THEY?

STAN
You know... They.

KYLE
They're.. they're bastards.

KELLY
Well don't just stand there! Help him!

Now they look REALLY confused.

KYLE
What?

STAN
Help... him?

KELLY
(In disgust)
UGH!!

Kelly runs over to Kenny, pinches his nose,
and starts giving him mouth-to-mouth.

KELLY
Come on, Benny, breathe! Breathe you son of a BITCH!

Kelly pounds five times on Kenny's chest,
picking her nose quickly between the third
and fourth. Finally, we hear a COUGH.

We see only Kelly's face as she smiles.

PROD. # _____ 301
SC.

SC.

SC.

Scene 902	Panel	BG

Location/Time   Rev.

Dialogue

KELLY
WHAT?! WHO?! WHO KILLED HIM?!

Action/Efx

Have Kelly turn to camera in this shot.

Trans.

59

Scene 903	Panel	BG

Location/Time

Dialogue

STAN
THEY did.

Action/Efx

Stan and Kyle look confused.

Trans.

45

Scene 904	Panel	BG S/A 902

Location/Time   Rev.

Dialogue

KELLY
Who's THEY?

Action/Efx

Trans.

26

---

301   301

Scene 905	Panel	BG S/A 903

Location/Time

Dialogue

STAN
You know... They.

KYLE
They're bastards.

Thejre

Action/Efx

Trans.

94

Scene 906		BG S/A 902

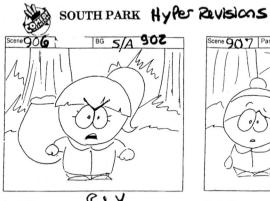

Location/Time   REV

Dialogue

KELLY
Well don't just stand there! Help him!

Action/Efx

Trans.

46

Scene 907	Panel	BG S/A 903

Location/Time

Dialogue

KYLE
What?

STAN
Help... him?

Action/Efx

Now they look REALLY confused.

Trans.

42

KYLE
(Amazed)
Whoa, dude!

EXT. RAINFOREST PEACE SUMMIT

The kids are up on the stage singing to the huge audience.

ANNOUNCER
And now, here to teach us about the
rainforest is GETTING GAY WITH KIDS!!!

The curtain opens, revealing the
kids and the choir teacher.

CHOIR TEACHER
Does everybody have the new lyrics?

They nod.

CHOIR TEACHER (cont'd)
And -

KIDS
(singing)
Doo Doo Doo Doo Doo. Zat A Doot A Waa.
There is a place called the rainforest
that truly sucks ass. Let's knock it
all down and get rid of it fast.
You say 'Save the Rainforest,' but what do you know?
You've never been to the rainforest before.
Getting Gay With Kids is here!
To tell you things you might not like to hear.
You only fight these causes because caring sells.
All of you actors can go fuck yourselves.

They continue their anti-rainforest song. We reveal that
both Kelly AND Kenny are there. Kelly smiles at him.

The crowd goes wild.

MAN
That was so inspiring!

WOMAN
What a wonderful message!

KIDS
(singing)
Someday if you work hard boys and girls
There'll be nothing but rainforest
covering the entire world.
Getting Gay With Kids is here!
To spread the word and bring you cheer.
Getting Gay With Kids is here!
To help save the rainforest, what do you say?
It's totally gay! It's totally gay!

TITLES come up over black, one fading into the next.

Each year, the rainforest is responsible for over three
thousand deaths from accidents, attacks or illnesses.

There are over seven hundred things in the
rainforest that cause cancer.

Join the fight now and help stop the
rainforest before it's too late.

END.